SKIATHOS

THE UPDATED TRAVEL GUIDE

Discover the Allure of Skiathos: The Ultimate Vacation Guide to Greece's Extraordinary Island, Discover the Finest of Beaches, Attractions, and Retreats in the Sporades

John Schnell

Copyright © [2023] by [John Schnell]

All rights reserved. No part of this publication may be reproduced, distributed, or transmitted in any form or by any means, including photocopying, recording, or other electronic or mechanical methods, without the prior written permission of the author, except in the case of brief quotations embodied in critical reviews and certain other non-commercial uses permitted by copyright law

TABLE OF CONTENTS

TABLE OF CONTENTS 3

INTRODUCTION 7

WELCOME TO SKIATHOS 11

    Location and Geography 11

    History 13

    Weather and Climate 16

INTERESTING THINGS THAT MAKE SKIATHOS UNIQUE FOR TRAVELERS 20

VISA REQUIREMENTS 24

BEST TIME TO VISIT 26

    Travel Experience in Skiathos by Season 26

SOME CULTURAL CUSTOMS AND ETIQUETTE TO KNOW 29

    Other Things You Should Know 33

SOME USEFUL PHRASES AND VOCABULARY TO UNDERSTAND 36

GETTING TO SKIATHOS 40

TRAVELING AROUND SKIATHOS 43

COST OF A TRIP TO SKIATHOS 45

MONEY-SAVING TIPS FOR BUDGET TRAVELERS. 49

THINGS TO BRING ON A TRIP 53

HEALTH AND SAFETY ADVICE 58

POPULAR SCAMS TO BE AWARE OF 62

SOME POPULAR ATTRACTIONS IN SKIATHOS 68

    Bourtzi 68

    Sea caves 69

    Medieval Castle 72

    Monastery of Evangelistria 73

    Biotope 75

    House of Papadiamantis 77

    Monastery of Panagia Kounistra 79

    Church of Three Bishops 81

    Church of Agios Nikolaos 83

SOME OFF-THE-BEATEN-PATH LOCATIONS IN SKIATHOS 85

NEARBY DAY TRIPS FROM SKIATHOS 88

OUTDOOR ACTIVITIES IN SKIATHOS 92

A PERFECT SEVEN-DAY ITINERARY FOR A VISIT TO SKIATHOS 97

Day 1: Arrival and Beach Time 97
Day 2: Sailing Adventure 97
Day 3: Trekking and Exploration 98
Day 4: Day Trip to Skopelos 98
Day 5: Water Sports and Evening Stroll 99
Day 6: Relaxation and Sunset Watching 99
Day 7: Biking and Farewell 100

CULTURAL FESTIVALS AND HOLIDAYS 101

BEST BEACHES IN SKIATHOS 107

SKIATHOS FOR FAMILIES 114

Family-Friendly Activities and Experiences 114

SKIATHOS FOR COUPLES 119

SHOPPING AND DINING 125

Local Cuisines and Specialties 125

Popular Restaurants and Cafes 131

Shopping Districts and Markets 136

Souvenirs and Local Products 140

NIGHTLIFE IN SKIATHOS 144

Best Bars and Nightclubs 144

ACCOMMODATION OPTIONS 150

Budget-Friendly Accommodation 150

Luxury Hotels and Resorts 153

Camping and Alternative Accommodations 155

BEST TRAVEL RESOURCES 159

CONCLUSION 161

INTRODUCTION

As I stepped off the plane onto the sun-drenched tarmac of Skiathos Airport, a warm breeze greeted me, carrying the subtle scent of sea salt and pine. The anticipation of a week-long holiday on this picturesque Greek island had been building within me for months, and now, surrounded by the azure waters of the Aegean Sea, I felt an immediate sense of tranquility settle over me.

Skiathos, known for its stunning beaches, vibrant nightlife, and lush landscapes, had always been a dream destination for me. My first glimpse of the island did not disappoint; the coastal town, with its white-washed buildings and terracotta rooftops, radiated a sense of charm that was both inviting and calming.

My accommodation was a cozy villa nestled amidst olive groves and fragrant pine trees. From the moment I stepped into the villa, I was struck by the breathtaking view it offered. A sprawling balcony opened up to a panorama of the sea, the horizon painted with hues of gold and orange as the sun began its descent. Each morning, I would wake up to the gentle sounds of the waves and the melodies of chirping birds, an idyllic symphony that set the tone for the day.

The first order of business was to explore the island's renowned beaches. Koukounaries, often dubbed the "Golden Sand Beach," lived up to its reputation. The soft sand stretched out like a warm invitation, and the crystal-clear waters were a haven for swimming and relaxation. The feeling of the sun's warmth on my skin and the refreshing sea breeze made me realize I had found paradise.

Venturing into Skiathos Town, I was charmed by its labyrinthine streets lined with boutiques, cafes, and tavernas. The aroma of freshly baked pastries and local delicacies filled the air. As I strolled through the town, I stumbled upon hidden squares adorned with vibrant flowers and shaded by ancient trees, perfect spots to sit and people-watch while sipping on a strong Greek coffee.

One of the highlights of my trip was a day-long sailing excursion around the island. Aboard a traditional wooden boat, I sailed along the rugged coastline, exploring hidden coves and sea caves. The cerulean waters sparkled under the sun's gaze, and the captain's tales of local folklore and history added an enriching layer to the experience.

Evenings in Skiathos were a delightful blend of relaxation and entertainment. Dinners in waterfront tavernas consisted of fresh seafood, grilled vegetables, and local wines. As the sun dipped below the horizon, the town transformed into a lively hub of activity. Music and laughter filled the air as I joined in the festivities, dancing under the starlit sky with both locals and fellow travelers.

As my holiday in Skiathos drew to a close, I found myself reflecting on the moments of serenity and adventure that had defined my visit. The island had offered a perfect balance of relaxation and exploration, leaving me rejuvenated and inspired. Whether it was the mesmerizing beauty of its beaches, the warmth of its people, or the rich tapestry of its culture, Skiathos had woven an unforgettable chapter into the fabric of my travel experiences.

With a heavy heart and a camera full of memories, I bid farewell to this enchanting island. As the plane took off, I looked out at the receding coastline, vowing to return someday to relive the magic of Skiathos and create new memories that would last a lifetime.

WELCOME TO SKIATHOS

Location and Geography

Skiathos constitutes a member of the cluster of Greek islands referred to as the Sporades, situated to the northwest of Evia island. Positioned between the coastal regions of Magnesia to the west and the island of Skopelos to the east, its historical roots are closely intertwined with its neighboring areas. Skiathos is bounded by the Skiathos Channel on its western front and the Skopelos Channel on its eastern border. The island spans an area of 61 square kilometers, with dimensions of 12 kilometers in length and 6 kilometers in width from its northern to southern points, encompassing a total perimeter of 48 kilometers.

The geographical aspect of Skiathos is defined by its flourishing wooded zones and crystalline waters, which collectively present an abundance of natural magnificence. The majority of the island is characterized by mountains, the highest pinnacle being Stavros, ascending to an elevation of 433 meters atop the northern mountain named Karafiltzanaka. Skiathos boasts numerous coastlines, bays, inlets, and peninsulas. The northwestern region, due to its ruggedness, remains largely inaccessible and is home to the cape known as Kastro.

In contrast, the southeastern section of the island offers a distinct ambiance – tranquil and serene. Here lies Skiathos Town, the island's capital and harbor, positioned on the western expanse of the bay bearing the same name. The capes of Sozon and Gournes delineate the bay of Katavothras in the west, while the cape of Pounta shapes the well-known sandy beaches of Koukounaries and Platanias in the southwest. Towards the island's northern flank, a plethora of exquisite caves are scattered, reachable solely by boat.

With an approximate population of 5,000 residents, a majority of whom reside in the capital, Skiathos sustains its economy chiefly through tourism and fishing activities, with agriculture taking a backseat. Much akin to its counterparts in the Sporades, Skiathos is heavily wooded, adorned with pine, plane, oak, and olive trees, as well as a variety of plant species. The eastern portion of the island, predominantly forested, is ecologically safeguarded, as its uniqueness has earned it recognition across Greece as a rare habitat demanding vigilant conservation efforts.

History

Skiathos has retained its name since the pre-Hellenic era, believed to be bestowed upon the island by its initial inhabitants, the Pelasgians. Their choice of name is attributed to the abundant tree cover casting impressive shadows ("skia" in Greek). The island revered Dionysus as its deity. Following this early settlement phase, Cretans and Mycenaeans, who also occupied other Sporades islands, became successive inhabitants of Skiathos. The island's fertility and strategic location lured numerous invaders.

During the periods of the 7th and 6th centuries BC, inhabitants of Chalkis on the island of Evia undertook the colonization of Skiathos, leading to the establishment of the inaugural fortified settlement on the island. Skiathos proved invaluable to Athenians during the Persian Wars, utilizing its harbor as a naval base. By 478 BC, Skiathos joined the Athenian Delian League. After the Peloponnesian War (404 BC), the island gained official autonomy and independence. Although Spartans sought to reclaim Skiathos, its populace, aided by Athenians, successfully expelled them, securing peace and autonomy for four decades.

The island's prosperity waned when Athens transformed it into a military outpost against Philip II of Macedonia. Subsequently captured by the Macedonians, Skiathos endured tyrannical rule until democracy was reinstated in 341 BC. In the wake of Alexander the Great's death, Greece and Skiathos witnessed a succession of leaders, leading to considerable hardships. In 197 BC, Skiathos reclaimed its democracy.

Roman rule gripped Greece in 146 BC, granting certain freedoms to Skiathos residents who existed peacefully under Roman rule. However, in 88 BC, King Mithriades VI of Pontus razed Skiathos during his conflict with Rome. In 42 BC, Skiathos reverted to Athenian dominion, but pirate raids plagued the island during this period. After 221 AD, Roman control resumed, coinciding with the growth and development of the island's town.

Medieval Era

Christianity took root on Skiathos in 325 AD, with the first church dedicated to the Holy Trinity constructed in 530. In the time of the Byzantine period, Skiathos was situated within the jurisdiction of Thessaly province. The bishop of the island was associated with the Metropolis of Larissa. In the 7th century, Saracen pirates devastated the island, similar to their actions across the Aegean Sea. In 1204, Crusaders obtained dominion over the Aegean Islands, including Skiathos, subsequently passing control to the Venetians.

The Venetians erected a castle, now called Bourtzi, in the island's main port. The Ghisi family ruled Skiathos until 1276, after which the island changed hands among other Venetians, remaining under their influence until Constantinople's fall in 1453.

Ottoman Rule and Independence

In 1538 AD, the Ottomans asserted control over Skiathos. During the early 19th century, the islanders delved into shipbuilding. Well-prepared for the War of Independence, the locals actively participated in revolutionary actions against the Turks. Skiathos provided refuge for Greek revolutionaries, as well as British, Australian, and New Zealand soldiers during the Nazi occupation.

Recent History

Post the Greek Revolution, the town of Kastro was abandoned in favor of a new settlement near the port. Boatbuilding resumed, and Skiathos inspired artists and writers, including Alexandros Papadiamantis and Alexandros Moraitidis. During World War II, the town endured significant damage from German bombs during the Nazi occupation.

The sinking of the Greek submarine Lambros Katsonis near Skiathos' shores on September 14th, 1943, is annually commemorated through the Katsonia Festival. Kastro became a sanctuary for Greek revolutionaries and Allied soldiers during the occupation. After the war, Skiathos experienced rapid economic and social development.

Weather and Climate

A Mediterranean climate characterizes Skiathos, with warm, sunny summers and milder, wetter winters. The physical position of the island—it is surrounded by water—as well as the atmospheric patterns of the Mediterranean region—have a significant impact on the weather and climate of the island.

Summer (June–August): Sunny skies and mild to hot temperatures define Skiathos' summer season. The typical high temperature is between 28°C and 32°C (82°F and 89°F), however, there are occasional heatwaves that raise the temperature much higher.

The sea is a comfortable temperature for swimming, often between 24°C and 26°C (75°F and 79°F). It is the busiest travel season since there is seldom rain and the sky is often clear. Beautiful beaches in Skiathos are popular with tourists who come to relax in the Mediterranean sun and partake in a variety of water sports.

Autumn (September to November): Skiathos has lower temperatures in the fall, making it a great time to visit if you want to escape the busiest summer months. The weather is still good and the water is still warm in September, with highs about 26°C (79°F) and dropping as the season goes on. Gradually more rain falls, and storms may appear sometimes.

Visitors may enjoy locally grown fruits and vegetables including figs, grapes, and olives since it is also harvest season.

Winter (December–February): Skiathos have comparatively moderate winters when compared to more northern climes, although they are also colder and wetter than the summertime.

Lows typically vary from 7°C to 10°C (45°F to 50°F), with average highs of 11° to 14°C (52° to 57°F). During this time, rain falls more often, and while it is uncommon, snowfall sometimes occurs in higher altitudes. The island preserves its own character and provides a calmer experience for those who want a peaceful getaway, even if some shops may shut down during this off-peak season.

Spring (March–May): As the island wakes from its winter sleep, spring is a fantastic time to visit Skiathos. As the temperature rises, the foliage begins to change color and become more colorful. Highs typically range from 15°C to 20°C (59°F to 68°F), which is comfortable for outdoor activities. Early in the season, the water may still be a little cool for swimming even if the temperature is starting to rise. Spring also brings sporadic rains, which add to the island's verdant scenery.

General Climate

Due to the island's closeness to the ocean, summers are neither as hot or as cold as they could otherwise be.

During the summer, the Meltemi breezes, which usually blow from the north, may have a cooling effect, making the heat more bearable.

The island's lush foliage during the colder months and its parched landscapes during the summer months are both products of the island's unique wet and dry seasons in the Mediterranean climate.

While summer is the busiest season for visitors, spring and fall provide warmer temperatures and less congestion, making them perfect for a relaxing and delightful trip.

INTERESTING THINGS THAT MAKE SKIATHOS UNIQUE FOR TRAVELERS

Here are some intriguing insights about Skiathos.

While the name 'Skiathos' might not immediately ring a bell, movie enthusiasts will be fascinated to discover that the acclaimed film 'Mamma Mia' was actually filmed on this island. Travelers flock to Skiathos to explore the locations where this remarkable movie was created.

Skiathos is a part of the island cluster known as the Sporades. The term 'Sporades' translates to 'the scattered ones,' referring to the Aegean archipelago that lies beyond the Cyclades. Among the 24 islands that make up the Sporades, only four, including Skiathos, are inhabited. This subgroup is also referred to as the Thessalian Sporades.

Skiathos Island played a noteworthy, albeit minor, role during the conflict between Persia and the 300 Spartans. Xerxes, the Persian king, faced a significant storm along the island's coast, disrupting his fleet. In response, the

Greek fleet blocked the surrounding waters to prevent the Persian forces from advancing, resulting in the Persians' defeat.

In the 19th century, **Greece's inaugural flag** was designed and raised at the Evangelistria Monastery in Skiathos. Distinguished Greeks and religious figures attended this significant event.

During the 1900s, the island emerged as a thriving hub for **ship construction**. The ships were crafted from wood sourced from the island's dominant pine forests. Even today, a small shipyard located in the northern part of the island's town continues to construct caiques, traditional Greek boats.

The island's **spectacular beaches** are a true wonder. Adorned with the greenery of pine and plane trees that embrace every cove and settlement, Skiathos' beaches are a sight to behold. They feature inviting, warm turquoise waters, shaded by lush pine forests that sometimes extend right up to the water's edge. In several instances, the beaches are complemented by rich wetlands.

Skiathos served as the inspiration for the renowned short story writer **Alexandros Papadiamantis**. Beyond being a major attraction on the island, the fact that such a prominent Greek personality hailed from Skiathos motivates exploration, inviting visitors to uncover what made the island uniquely influential in shaping both his works and way of life.

Marine Diversity: The waters surrounding Skiathos teem with a diverse array of marine life, attracting diving and snorkeling enthusiasts. Visitors have the opportunity to venture into underwater caves and witness the vibrant marine ecosystem.

Preservation of Ecosystem: The island's ecosystem, particularly its eastern side, holds ecological importance and is safeguarded by Greek regulations. This region hosts rare plant species, transforming it into a valuable ecological habitat that necessitates meticulous conservation efforts.

An abundance of Greenery: Despite its Mediterranean climate, Skiathos is astonishingly verdant due to its lush pine forests, olive groves, and diverse plant species. The island's natural splendor is a defining attribute that beautifully complements its captivating beaches.

Scenic Beaches: Skiathos may be petite, but it boasts an impressive array of over 60 breathtaking beaches, each with its own distinct character. Among these, Koukounaries Beach stands out with its golden sands and crystal-clear waters. Lalaria Beach, accessible exclusively by boat, is famous for its unique white pebbles and captivating sea caves.

VISA REQUIREMENTS

Citizens of most nations, including the United States, Canada, Australia, New Zealand, and most European countries, do not need a visa to visit Greece for tourist reasons. There are a few outliers, such as Afghans, Iranians, Iraqis, Pakistanis, and Syrians. On the website of the Greek Ministry of Foreign Affairs, you can find a comprehensive list of countries that need a visa to visit Greece.

If you want a visa, you may get one through a Greek embassy or consulate in your home country. The application procedure usually takes a few weeks, so apply well in advance of your departure date. A valid passport, a completed visa application form, a current passport-sized picture, and evidence of financial assistance are all required.

You will be eligible to enter Greece for up to three months after you have obtained your visa. If you want to remain for an extended period of time, you must apply for a residence permit.

A valid passport valid for at least three months beyond the end of your planned stay in Greece is required in addition to a visa. You should also have a return ticket or other means of transportation.

If you are coming to Greece from a nation that is not a Schengen member, you must additionally fill out a Passenger Locator Form (PLF) before you leave. The PLF is available for completion online at the Greek government's website.

Please visit the Greek Ministry of Foreign Affairs website for further information on visa requirements for Greece. https://www.mfa.gr/en/visas/visas-for-foreigners-traveling-to-greece/

BEST TIME TO VISIT

The Most and Least Crowded Months

Skiathos, Greece experiences its peak tourist activity during June, followed by July and May. Accommodation and flight prices tend to be higher during these months, but booking in advance can lead to savings.

Conversely, October usually witnesses a decrease in tourist influx. Those open to visiting during this period are likely to find it the most cost-effective month for their trip.

Travel Experience in Skiathos by Season

Spring (March through May)

During spring, the combination of humidity and temperatures creates a moderate climate. High temperatures range from 76.1°F (24.5°C) to 55.9°F (13.3°C), with warmer conditions in the later spring months.

Rainfall is infrequent, with significant precipitation occurring on 2 to 4 days per month. Spring ranks as the second busiest tourist season, making it an optimal time for those seeking various activities.

Summer (June through August)

The middle months of the year offer very pleasant weather, featuring comfortably high temperatures. Precipitation during this period is minimal, with 0 to 2 days of rain per month. June to August constitutes Skiathos' peak tourist season, resulting in potentially higher costs for lodging and accommodations compared to other times.

Fall (September through November)

Autumn's daily highs span from 80°F (26.7°C) to 62.5°F (16.9°C), providing a very pleasant experience due to manageable humidity and winds. Rain or snowfall is typical, averaging 2 to 4 days per month.

These months experience slower tourism due to weather conditions, which often leads to more affordable hotel prices.

Winter (December through February)

The weather during winter in Skiathos is too cold to be comfortable for travelers seeking warmer conditions. The average high temperatures range from 60.3°F (15.7°C) to 53.5°F (11.9°C). On average, there are 5 to 7 instances of rain or snowfall per month.

These seasons typically see a decrease in tourist activity due to the climate.

SOME CULTURAL CUSTOMS AND ETIQUETTE TO KNOW

When visiting Skiathos it's important to respect and embrace the local culture and customs. Here are some key cultural customs and etiquettes to keep in mind during your stay:

Greetings and Politeness:

Greeks are generally warm and friendly people. When meeting someone, a handshake is common, and close friends might greet each other with a hug and a kiss on both cheeks.

Use "Kalimera" (good morning), "Kalispera" (good evening), and "Kalinihta" (good night) as appropriate greetings throughout the day.

When addressing people, it's polite to use their titles and last names, especially in formal settings.

Dress Code:

When visiting churches and monasteries, both men and women should dress modestly. Refrain from putting on shorts, sleeveless tops, and attire that exposes a lot of skin.

For casual settings, comfortable and modest clothing is acceptable, especially when you're exploring the island.

Table Manners:

When dining, it's customary to say "Kali Oreksi" (good appetite) before starting your meal.

Greeks often share dishes, so it's common for meals to be communal experiences. Feel free to experiment with a diverse selection of culinary offerings.

It's polite to finish your plate as it's considered wasteful to leave food.

Tipping:

Tipping is appreciated in restaurants, cafes, and bars. It's customary to leave around 5-10% of the bill as a tip.

Public Behavior:

Public displays of affection should be kept moderate, as overt displays might be considered inappropriate.

Refrain from elevating your vocal tone or exhibiting signs of anger in public settings. Greeks value calm and composed interactions.

Beach Etiquette:

When at the beach, appropriate swimwear is essential. It's customary to use a cover-up when walking away from the beach or entering a nearby establishment.

Respect the environment by cleaning up after yourself and not leaving trash on the beach.

Gift Giving:

When invited to someone's home, it's a thoughtful gesture to bring a small gift for the host. Local products like wine, olive oil, or pastries are great choices.

Religious Sites:

When visiting churches or monasteries, be respectful and quiet. Dress modestly, and if there's a service in progress, avoid walking around and taking photos.

Time Flexibility:

Greeks tend to have a relaxed attitude toward time. While punctuality is valued in formal settings, social gatherings might start a bit later than planned.

Bargaining and Shopping:

Bargaining isn't common in shops, as most prices are fixed. However, at local markets and open-air stalls, a bit of friendly negotiation might be possible.

Smoking Regulations:

Greece has regulations about smoking in public places. Make sure to follow the designated smoking areas to respect non-smokers.

Other Things You Should Know

When interacting with the inhabitants of Skiathos, it's important to be aware of their distinct gestures and behaviors. For instance, it's best to avoid mimicking the action of brushing off dust from a lapel, as this can be seen as disrespectful. Locals might interpret it as an insult.

When the people of Skiathos want to indicate a negative response, they tend to raise their eyebrows and their head while gently clicking their tongues. A gesture that signifies "come here" involves extending their arms with palms facing downward. Additionally, Greeks often touch their lower lip with their index finger to indicate that they have something to share.

Skiathos locals are known for their penchant to interrupt conversations, raise their voices, and make physical contact during discourse. Expressing emotions openly is a common trait among the inhabitants. It's not unusual to witness someone spontaneously burst into song while in a park or on public transportation. During meals, Greeks engage in continuous chatter and laughter, and it's not uncommon for a plate of food to be playfully turned over. In short, adherence to traditional etiquette might not be as strict among the locals. An invitation to a Greek's home may not necessarily entail a meal.

Community members of Skiathos enjoy congregating at their favorite taverns with family and friends. Here, they partake in local beverages, share meals, and engage in conversation accompanied by folk music and dancing. However, it's worth noting that encountering intoxicated individuals on the streets of Skiathos is uncommon. This is because Greeks, both locals, and visitors, view such behavior as disgraceful. To avoid negative judgments, maintaining self-control is advisable.

Furthermore, it's respectful to dress modestly and refrain from strolling in a bikini along the streets of Skiathos. Particularly in conservative villages, the locals uphold traditional values.

To win the favor of a Greek individual, offering positive remarks about Skiathos or demonstrating knowledge of historical facts about Greece can be quite effective. Greeks exhibit strong patriotism while often voicing critiques about their government.

However, it's important for foreigners to refrain from expressing similar criticisms. Locals tend to be uncomfortable when outsiders speak unfavorably about Greece. In Skiathos, it's customary to greet anyone entering a public space, be it a shop or a tavern.

Greeks have a propensity for offering advice and imparting moral lessons, a tendency that often intensifies with age. Nevertheless, the elderly are held in high regard within the community. Many Greeks continue to live with their parents until the age of thirty. Men in the region are known for their flirtatious nature and penchant for complimenting women. This behavior remains unchanged even in the presence of their wife or girlfriend.

SOME USEFUL PHRASES AND VOCABULARY TO UNDERSTAND

Learning some basic Greek expressions can greatly enrich your experience on the island and allow you to connect more effectively with locals. Here's a breakdown of essential phrases and vocabulary for various situations:

Greetings and Basic Phrases:

Hello / Hi: Γειά σας (Yia sas)

Good morning: Καλημέρα (Kalimera)

Good afternoon: Καλησπέρα (Kalispera)

Good evening: Καλησπέρα (Kalispera)

Goodnight: Καληνύχτα (Kalinichta)

Goodbye: Αντίο (Adio)

Please: Παρακαλώ (Parakalo)

Thank you: Ευχαριστώ (Efharisto)

Yes: Ναι (Ne)

No: Όχι (Ochi)

Getting Around:

Where is...?: Πού είναι...; (Pou ine...?)

How much is this?: Πόσο κοστίζει αυτό; (Poso kostizi afto?)

I would like...: Θα ήθελα... (Tha ithela...)

How do I get to...?: Πώς πάω στο...; (Pos pao sto...?)

Can you help me?: Μπορείτε να με βοηθήσετε; (Borite na me voithisete?)

I don't understand: Δεν καταλαβαίνω (Den katalavaino)

Excuse me: Συγγνώμη (Siggnomi)

Eating and Drinking:

Menu: Μενού (Menu)

Water: Νερό (Nero)

Coffee: Καφές (Kafes)

Tea: Τσάι (Tsai)

Breakfast: Πρωινό (Proino)

Lunch: Μεσημεριανό (Mesimeriano)

Dinner: Δείπνο (Dipno)

Bill, please: Το λογαριασμό, παρακαλώ (To logariasmo, parakalo)

Directions and Transportation:

Bus station: Στάση λεωφορείου (Stasi leoforeiou)

Taxi: Ταξί (Taksi)

Airport: Αεροδρόμιο (Aerodromio)

Harbor / Port: Λιμάνι (Limani)

Hotel: Ξενοδοχείο (Xenodohio)

Beach: Παραλία (Paralia)

Street: Οδός (Odos)

Left: Αριστερά (Aristera)

Right: Δεξιά (Dexia)

Straight ahead: Κατευθείαν (Katefthian)

Emergency and Health:

Help!: Βοήθεια! (Voithia!)

Doctor: Γιατρός (Yiatros)

Hospital: Νοσοκομείο (Nosokomeio)

Police: Αστυνομία (Astynomia)

I need a pharmacy: Χρειάζομαι μια φαρμακείο (Hriazome mia farmakeio)

I am not feeling well: Δεν αισθάνομαι καλά (Den aisthanome kala)

Cultural Insights:

What is this called?: Πώς λέγεται αυτό; (Pos legetai afto?)

Can you tell me about this place?: Μπορείτε να μου πείτε γι' αυτόν τον τόπο; (Borite na mou pite yi' afton ton topo?)

By familiarizing yourself with these phrases and vocabulary, you'll not only make your trip to Skiathos more enjoyable but also show respect for the local culture and enhance your interactions with the friendly residents. Remember, even attempting a few words in the local language can go a long way in creating positive and memorable experiences.

GETTING TO SKIATHOS

Getting to Skiathos is an exciting journey that offers various transportation options. Whether you're arriving by air, sea, or land, each route presents its own charm and convenience. Here's a comprehensive guide on how to get to Skiathos:

1. By Air:

The quickest and most convenient way to reach Skiathos is by air. Skiathos Island National Airport (JSI) serves as the main gateway for travelers. Here's how to get there:

Domestic Flights: Numerous domestic flights connect Athens International Airport (ATH) with Skiathos Airport. Flight duration is approximately 40-50 minutes. Various airlines offer daily flights during the peak tourist season.

International Connections: While Skiathos Airport is primarily a domestic airport, some international charters and seasonal flights are available, especially during the summer months. Some common international connections include flights from the United Kingdom, Germany, and other European countries.

2. By Sea:

If you prefer a more leisurely journey with the opportunity to admire the stunning Greek coastline, traveling to Skiathos by ferry or boat is an excellent choice:

Ferries: Ferries and high-speed catamarans operate from Volos, Agios Konstantinos, and Kimi on the mainland, as well as from nearby islands like Skopelos and Alonissos. Ferries offer a more scenic route, but the travel time can vary depending on the departure point and type of vessel.

Ferry Operators: Companies like Hellenic Seaways, Anes Ferries, and Aegean Flying Dolphins operate ferry services to Skiathos. Some ferries are slower but more economical, while high-speed options are quicker but might be slightly more expensive.

Cruises: Skiathos is also a popular stop for cruise ships and yacht charters. This offers a luxurious way to arrive at the island while enjoying the amenities of the vessel.

3. By Land and Sea Combination:

For those seeking a mix of transportation experiences, you can combine land and sea travel:

Drive and Ferry: You can drive to one of the mainland ports like Volos, Agios Konstantinos, or Kimi and take a ferry to Skiathos. This option allows you to explore the mainland before embarking on a maritime adventure.

TRAVELING AROUND SKIATHOS

Public Transportation Options

Exploring the region through public transportation is both cost-effective and an enjoyable way to discover the area!

Skiathos boasts relatively frequent bus itineraries compared to other islands. The central bus station, situated in Chora, serves as the starting point for three distinct bus lines that lead to Koukounaries, Xanemos, and the Evangelistria Monastery.

Taxis and Private Transfers

While taxis may incur higher costs in comparison to buses, they offer a convenient and swift mode of transportation to your chosen destination. Taxis are typically available at central locations.

Car and Motorcycle Rentals

Opting for a car or motorcycle empowers you to explore the island on your terms and access its most secluded corners. If you lack personal transportation, renting a vehicle is an excellent solution for your sightseeing adventures. Given Skiathos' relatively compact size, renting a motorcycle might be a more suitable choice.

Organized Excursions

Embarking on organized tours can provide you with unforgettable experiences, such as journeys to the island's secluded beaches and the stunning coastline of Skiathos. Additionally, boat trips to the uninhabited Tsougria Island are frequently arranged during the summer season.

Water Taxis

Water taxis present an alternative means of traversing Skiathos and reaching neighboring destinations. If you require a water taxi, it's advisable to prearrange your transfer for a seamless experience.

COST OF A TRIP TO SKIATHOS

The cost of a trip to Skiathos, like any travel destination, can vary widely based on factors such as your travel style, preferences, and the time of year you visit. Here's a detailed breakdown of the potential expenses you might encounter when planning a trip to Skiathos:

1. Flights:

Flight costs will depend on your departure location, time of booking, and whether you're flying during peak or off-peak seasons.

Domestic flights within Greece from Athens to Skiathos can range from approximately $100 to $300 round trip per person.

International flights from other countries might vary greatly in price, but you could expect to pay between $300 to $800 or more, depending on your departure location and the time of year.

2. Accommodation:

Hotel rates can vary significantly depending on the type of accommodation you choose, the location, and the time of year.

Budget accommodations (hostels, guesthouses): $30 - $80 per night.

Mid-range hotels: $80 - $150 per night.

Luxury resorts: $150 - $400+ per night.

3. Meals and Dining:

Meals at local tavernas and cafes: $10 - $30 per person per meal.

Dining at upscale restaurants: $30 - $60+ per person per meal.

Food costs can vary based on whether you choose local specialties or international cuisine.

4. Transportation on the Island:

Public buses: Around $2 per ride.

Taxi rides: Starting at around $5 and varying based on distance.

Car rental: Approximately $40 - $80 per day, depending on the type of vehicle.

Motorcycle or scooter rental: Around $20 - $40 per day.

5. Activities and Entertainment:

Entrance fees to museums or historical sites: $5 - $15 per person.

Water sports and activities: Costs vary based on the activity, but expect to pay around $20 - $50 per activity.

6. Excursions and Tours:

Organized boat tours: Prices vary depending on the type and length of the tour, ranging from $20 - $100 or more per person.

7. Miscellaneous Expenses:

Souvenirs and shopping: Costs vary based on personal preferences.

Tips: Tipping in restaurants and for services is customary and usually amounts to around 5-10% of the bill.

8. Travel Insurance:

Costs for travel insurance can vary but generally range from 5% to 10% of your total trip cost.

Total Estimated Cost:

On average, a mid-range budget traveler might spend around $80 - $150 per day, including accommodation, meals, transportation, and activities.

A more luxurious traveler might spend around $150 - $300+ per day.

Keep in mind that these are just estimated ranges, and the actual costs can vary widely based on individual choices, preferences, and unforeseen expenses. Researching and planning ahead will help you budget more accurately for your trip to Skiathos.

MONEY-SAVING TIPS FOR BUDGET TRAVELERS

For budget travelers, Skiathos can be an enchanting destination without breaking the bank. With careful planning and a few savvy strategies, you can make the most of your trip while keeping costs under control. Here are some detailed money-saving tips to consider:

1. Travel During Off-Peak Seasons:

Consider visiting Skiathos during the shoulder seasons of spring (April to June) and fall (September to October). Accommodation prices are often lower, and you'll enjoy fewer crowds at popular attractions.

2. Accommodation:

Opt for budget-friendly accommodations like guesthouses, hostels, or small local inns.

Look for deals on booking websites and compare prices before making reservations.

3. Eating Economically:

Dine at local tavernas and cafes, where you'll find authentic Greek dishes at more reasonable prices compared to upscale restaurants.

Try "set menu" options that offer a selection of dishes for a fixed price.

Consider getting some groceries from local markets or supermarkets and preparing simple meals if you have access to a kitchenette.

4. Transportation:

Utilize the local bus system to get around the island. Bus rides are affordable and provide easy access to major towns and beaches.

Consider renting a scooter or a bicycle, which can be cheaper than renting a car and give you a sense of freedom to explore.

5. Free and Low-Cost Activities:

Spend time at the beautiful beaches, most of which are free to access.

Explore walking trails and hiking routes, enjoying nature without any cost.

6. Discount Cards and Passes:

Look into any available discount cards or passes for attractions, public transportation, or museums that can save you money on entrance fees.

7. Plan Ahead:

Research and make a list of free or low-cost attractions and activities in advance.

Create a daily budget and stick to it as closely as possible.

8. Picnics and Local Markets:

Enjoy a picnic on the beach by buying fresh local produce, bread, and cheese from markets.

Explore nearby markets to find reasonably priced mementos and presents.

9. Water Activities:

Opt for less expensive water activities like snorkeling or renting basic kayaks instead of pricier options like jet skis or guided tours.

10. Avoid Peak Tourist Areas:

While these areas can be bustling with activity, they often come with higher price tags for dining and shopping.

Explore quieter neighborhoods and smaller towns for a more local and budget-friendly experience.

11. BYOB (Bring Your Own Bottle):

Bring a refillable water bottle to reduce the need to buy bottled water, which can add up over time.

12. Skip Guided Tours:

While organized tours can be convenient, they can also be costly. Instead, use maps and research to explore attractions on your own.

By implementing these money-saving tips, you can enjoy all that Skiathos has to offer without compromising your budget. Remember that budget travel is about making conscious choices and prioritizing experiences that align with your financial goals.

THINGS TO BRING ON A TRIP

When preparing for a vacation in Skiathos, it's crucial to pack thoughtfully to ensure you have all the necessary items while keeping your luggage manageable. Here's an extensive packing guide to help you organize your essentials:

Clothing:

Opt for Lightweight Attire: Choose breathable fabrics like cotton and linen to stay comfortable in the Mediterranean climate.

Pack Swimwear: Don't forget to bring swimsuits, cover-ups, and beach towels.

Comfortable Footwear: Include sandals, flip-flops, and walking shoes suitable for exploring.

Bring Light Jackets or Cardigans: Be prepared for cooler evenings and unexpected weather changes.

Protect Yourself: Don't forget a hat and sunglasses to shield yourself from the sun's rays.

Casual Outfits: Pack comfortable clothing suitable for beach days, sightseeing, and exploring the town.

Toiletries:

Sun Protection: Carry sunscreen with a high SPF to shield your skin from the intense sun.

Ward-Off Insects: Include insect repellent to prevent mosquito bites.

Essential Toiletries: Remember to pack items like a toothbrush, toothpaste, shampoo, conditioner, soap, and other personal necessities.

Medications: If you have any prescription medications, bring an adequate supply along with a basic first-aid kit.

Personal Hygiene: Don't forget deodorant, a hairbrush, and other hygiene items.

Electronics:

Keep Devices Charged: Pack your smartphone, charger, and a power bank to stay connected.

Capture Memories: Don't miss out on beautiful moments – bring a camera to capture the stunning landscapes.

Check Power Compatibility: If needed, bring adapters suitable for Greece's plug type.

Travel Essentials:

Important Documents: Safeguard your passport, ID, and travel-related papers in a secure travel pouch or wallet.

Travel Insurance: Carry copies of your policy information for reference.

Currency and Payment Options: Have both local currencies for smaller purchases and credit/debit cards for larger expenses.

Navigation Aids: Carry maps, guidebooks, and information about the island's attractions.

Travel Plans: Keep printed or digital copies of your itinerary and reservation details.

Miscellaneous Items:

Convenient Beach Bag: Ensure you have a bag to carry your beach essentials comfortably.

Stay Hydrated: Carry a reusable water bottle to both stay refreshed and reduce plastic waste.

Leisure Materials: Pack reading materials like books, magazines, or an e-reader for relaxing downtime.

Quick Snacks: Include some portable snacks for when you're on the go.

Lightweight Daypack: Having a daypack will come in handy for carrying essentials during day time.

Health and Safety:

Medication Preparedness: Bring enough prescription medications for your trip and carry a copy of the prescription.

Basic Medical Supplies: A small first-aid kit with band-aids, antiseptic wipes, and pain relievers is a practical addition.

Address Motion Sickness: If prone to motion sickness, consider bringing remedies for boat rides.

Allergy Support: Include allergy medications if you're sensitive to pollen or insects.

Entertainment and Comfort:

Comfortable Rest: Travel pillows aid in getting rest during transit.

Block out Distractions: Earplugs and an eye mask can help you rest during flights or in noisy accommodations.

Capture Memories: Carry a travel journal and pens to record your experiences and memories.

Downtime Entertainment: Bring books, magazines, or a tablet for leisurely moments.

As you pack, consider your specific requirements, planned activities, and the length of your stay. Checking the weather forecast closer to your departure date will help you make any necessary adjustments.

Efficient packing will ensure you have a comfortable and enjoyable experience during your holiday in Skiathos.

HEALTH AND SAFETY ADVICE

Traveling to Skiathos can be an incredible experience, but like any destination, it's important to prioritize your health and safety. Here's a detailed guide with health and safety advice for travelers in Skiathos:

1. Travel Insurance:

Ensure you have comprehensive travel insurance that covers medical expenses, trip cancellations, and unexpected emergencies.

Carry a copy of your insurance policy and contact information in case you need assistance.

2. Medical Preparations:

Before traveling, visit your doctor for a check-up and to discuss any necessary vaccinations or health precautions.

Pack a basic first-aid kit with items like band-aids, antiseptic wipes, pain relievers, and any prescription medications.

3. Stay Hydrated:

The Mediterranean climate can be hot and dry. Drink plenty of water throughout the day to stay hydrated, especially when spending time in the sun.

4. Sun Protection:

Protect your skin from the strong sun by wearing sunscreen with a high SPF, even on cloudy days.

Wear a wide-brimmed hat, sunglasses, and lightweight, long-sleeved clothing to minimize sun exposure.

5. Insect Protection:

Apply insect repellent to prevent mosquito bites, especially during the evening hours.

Keep doors and windows closed or use screens to keep insects out of your accommodations.

6. Food and Water Safety:

Stick to bottled water for drinking and brushing your teeth to avoid potential stomach issues.

Opt for freshly cooked and hot meals to reduce the risk of foodborne illnesses.

7. Beach Safety:

Follow posted signs and lifeguard instructions at the beaches.

Be cautious of strong currents, especially if you're not a confident swimmer.

8. Respect Local Customs:

Familiarize yourself with local customs and traditions to show respect for the local culture.

Dress modestly, especially when visiting religious sites.

9. Emergency Numbers:

Make a note of local emergency numbers, including those for medical assistance and the nearest embassy or consulate.

10. Medication and Medical Care:

If you have any medical conditions or allergies, wear a medical alert bracelet and carry the necessary medications.

Familiarize yourself with the location of local pharmacies and medical facilities.

11. Stay Updated:

Keep yourself updated with local news and travel advisories prior to and throughout your journey.

Be aware of any potential disruptions or safety concerns in the region.

12. Be Cautious with Alcohol:

Drink alcohol in a responsible manner and stay mindful of your environment.

Keep an eye on your drink to avoid any potential tampering.

13. Secure Valuables:

Use hotel safes to store passports, cash, and valuable items.

Avoid displaying expensive items like jewelry or electronics in crowded areas.

14. Safe Transportation:

If renting a vehicle, follow local traffic rules and drive cautiously.

Utilize trustworthy transportation providers and exercise vigilance while utilizing public transit options.

15. Respect the Environment:

Follow local regulations when participating in outdoor activities like hiking or water sports.

Avoid damaging the environment by not littering or disturbing wildlife.

POPULAR SCAMS TO BE AWARE OF

Tourist scams can be an unfortunate downside of traveling, along with the expenses. It's disheartening that some unscrupulous individuals take advantage of unsuspecting visitors who contribute to the local economy of the wonderful destinations they explore. Skiathos, Greece, is not exempt from these scams. Here's how to steer clear of tourist scams in Skiathos.

Camera Drop Scam

A common scam in Skiathos involves a local asking you to take their photo. They hand you their camera and request that you snap their picture. When you return the camera, they intentionally drop it, blaming you for damaging it, and insisting you pay for repairs. Politely decline taking anyone's photo unless you're absolutely certain they're not locals.

Taxi Overcharging

In places where services like Uber are unavailable, taxis are a necessity. Skiathos, Greece, is no exception. Always ensure that the taxi driver turns on the meter when you get in. It's also a good idea to plan your route before entering the taxi, so you have an estimated travel time. You can then ask the driver for an approximate duration and compare it to navigation apps like Google Maps or Waze on your phone.

ATM Assistance Scam

Beware of individuals offering help at ATM machines in Skiathos. They may approach you, claiming they can assist you in avoiding local bank fees. In reality, they aim to use a card skimmer to scan your debit or credit card and watch you enter your PIN, enabling them to access your account later. Another version involves them approaching when your card gets stuck in the ATM, offering assistance while actually aiming to steal your information. Ensure to shield the number pad as you input your PIN. Ideally, use credit cards with no foreign transaction fees and carry cash that can be exchanged at local banks in Skiathos.

Bar Scam

If your plans in Skiathos include socializing, be cautious of this scam. Two seemingly friendly individuals will engage you in conversation, suggesting mutual interest. They'll propose heading to a nearby bar (likely affiliated with them). After a few drinks, the bill will be exorbitant. They may offer to contribute a small amount, but if you don't pay, you might be escorted by bar staff to an ATM. To avoid this scam, suggest the bar yourself, and request the menu upon arrival to review prices.

Bird Poop Scam

A deceitful tactic involves someone throwing a white substance on your shoulder as you walk through Skiathos. Your natural reaction is to look up, thinking it's bird droppings. Suddenly, a "helpful" local offers assistance, cursing the birds for the mess. While cleaning you up, they also pickpocket you. Politely decline any "help" from locals who rush to your aid unless it's an emergency. Keep your belongings hidden, ideally in an internal pocket.

Guessing Game Scam

While strolling the streets of Skiathos, you might encounter a man with three boxes, a group of onlookers, and a guessing game involving a ball hidden within the boxes. Someone in the crowd guesses correctly and receives money as a reward. They repeat the scenario with another participant. The excitement draws more spectators.

Eventually, an innocent bystander is asked to guess, and in the midst of their focus, the group quickly pickpockets them for valuables. Stay cautious and avoid participating in such games or large crowds.

Fake Goods and Counterfeit Items:

Be cautious when shopping for designer brands or luxury items at significantly discounted prices. Some street vendors may offer counterfeit products that appear genuine but are of poor quality. Stick to well-established shops and authorized merchants.

Pickpocketing and Bag Snatching:

Crowded areas, public transportation, and tourist hotspots can be prime locations for pickpockets. Keep your belongings secure and avoid displaying valuable items such as expensive jewelry or electronics.

Unofficial Tour Guides:

Be cautious of individuals offering unsolicited tour guide services. They may provide inaccurate information and expect payment afterward. Opt for official tour guides recommended by reputable sources or travel agencies.

Fake Police Officers:

Scammers may pose as police officers to intimidate tourists into handing over money or valuables. Always ask for official identification, and if you have doubts, inform them that you'll verify their credentials with the local police station.

Fake Charity Requests:

Be wary of individuals asking for donations on the street or in crowded tourist areas. Some scammers may claim to be collecting money for charitable causes but keep the funds for themselves. If you wish to donate, do so through established, reputable charities.

Jewelry Scams:

Be cautious of street vendors selling jewelry or gemstones at seemingly low prices. Some may use fake or low-quality materials, misrepresent the value, or switch items when you're not looking. Purchase jewelry from established shops with a reputation for quality.

Ticket Scams:

Only purchase tickets for events, attractions, or transportation from authorized sellers. Scammers may sell fake tickets or overcharge tourists for admission to popular sites.

To protect yourself from these scams, it's essential to stay informed, use your common sense, and trust your instincts. Research your destination, be cautious of overly generous offers from strangers, and prioritize your safety at all times.

Being aware of these scams and practicing vigilance will help ensure a safe and enjoyable trip to Skiathos, Greece.

SOME POPULAR ATTRACTIONS IN SKIATHOS

Bourtzi

Bourtzi is a must-visit attraction for families on vacation in Skiathos. This charming historical site is sure to captivate both parents and children with its intriguing history and picturesque setting.

Bourtzi is a small, fortified islet located at the entrance of Skiathos harbor. It stands as a testament to the island's rich past and offers a unique opportunity for families to explore a piece of history while enjoying stunning views of the surrounding coastline.

Upon reaching Bourtzi, families will be greeted by the sight of the Venetian fortress that once served as protection against pirate attacks. The well-preserved stone walls, walkways, and turrets will transport you back in time, making it an engaging experience for children to imagine life in an ancient fortress.

For parents interested in history, Bourtzi offers informative plaques and displays that share insights into the fort's strategic significance and its role in safeguarding the island. Kids can learn about the Venetian influence on the region and the various events that shaped Skiathos' history.

One of the highlights for families visiting Bourtzi is the opportunity to climb up to the fortress's elevated points. As you ascend the stairs and reach the top, you'll be greeted by panoramic views of the sea, the harbor, and the surrounding landscape. It's an ideal spot for capturing memorable family photos and enjoying a moment of tranquility away from bustling tourist areas.

During your visit, you can take leisurely strolls along the pathways, exploring the fortress's nooks and crannies. Kids will enjoy the sense of adventure as they navigate through the historic structures. The islet's well-maintained gardens and shaded spots provide a serene setting to sit down for a family picnic or to rest while admiring the scenery.

Sea caves

For those seeking an extraordinary experience during their holiday in Skiathos, exploring the captivating sea caves that grace the island's coastline is an absolute must. These remarkable geological formations offer holidaymakers a unique opportunity to witness the sheer beauty and wonder of nature up close, adding an extra layer of excitement to their vacation.

Skiathos boasts a coastline adorned with stunning turquoise waters, and the sea caves enhance this beauty by offering a hidden world waiting to be discovered. Crafted over centuries by the ceaseless action of the waves, these caves exhibit intricate rock formations and secret passageways that beckon holidaymakers to embark on a journey of exploration and amazement.

To delve into this enchanting experience, visitors can choose guided boat tours or rent kayaks to navigate the sea caves. As you venture into these natural wonders, you'll be greeted by a magical interplay of sunlight filtering through openings and creating mesmerizing reflections on the water's surface. This interplay of light and shadow creates an ethereal atmosphere that holidaymakers will find utterly captivating.

Each sea cave in Skiathos possesses a distinct character, ranging from intimate chambers to more spacious caverns that invite you to uncover hidden treasures. Some caves even feature concealed alcoves and archways that lead to pockets of wonderment waiting to be explored. Discovering these caves is akin to stepping into a real-life fairy tale, awakening the sense of wonder in each holidaymaker.

For those who are comfortable swimming and snorkeling, some of the sea caves allow for a more immersive experience. The crystal-clear waters surrounding the caves provide an exceptional opportunity to witness vibrant marine life and an array of underwater landscapes, creating an unforgettable encounter with nature's underwater realm.

Safety is paramount when exploring sea caves, so it's crucial to heed the advice and instructions of experienced guides or boat operators. Wearing appropriate safety gear, such as life jackets, is essential to ensure a secure and enjoyable experience.

Ultimately, the sea caves of Skiathos offer an unparalleled blend of natural beauty and adventurous exploration for holidaymakers. With the guidance of knowledgeable locals or tour operators, visitors can embark on a journey that intertwines discovery, thrill, and the breathtaking allure of the island's coastline. When planning your holiday itinerary, make sure to include an exploration of the sea caves in Skiathos to create indelible memories surrounded by the island's awe-inspiring natural landscapes.

Medieval Castle

Perched atop a hill overlooking the charming town of Skiathos, the medieval castle stands as a testament to the island's historical significance and strategic importance. As holidaymakers approach the site, they'll be greeted by the impressive stone walls, towers, and arches that have withstood the test of time.

The castle's history dates back to the 14th century, a period characterized by the presence of Venetian and Ottoman influences in the region. Originally constructed by the Venetians as a defensive stronghold against pirate raids and invasions, the castle later passed into Ottoman hands. Its strategic location offered unparalleled views of the surrounding sea, enabling defenders to monitor the coastline and safeguard the island from potential threats.

Today, as visitors step within the castle's walls, they'll find themselves transported to an era of knights, battles, and medieval life. The remnants of buildings, towers, and pathways offer insights into the castle's layout and its historical significance. Families on holiday can explore the castle together, providing a learning opportunity for children and a chance to share the island's heritage.

As holidaymakers navigate the castle's narrow passages and climb its stone staircases, they'll be rewarded with panoramic views of Skiathos town, the sparkling Aegean Sea, and the lush landscape that surrounds the island. It's an ideal spot to capture stunning photographs, creating lasting memories of their visit.

Within the castle grounds, visitors will also find small exhibits or informational plaques that shed light on its history, providing context to the structures they encounter. Parents can share these stories with their children, making the experience both educational and engaging.

Monastery of Evangelistria

Nestled amidst the picturesque landscape of Skiathos, the Monastery of Evangelistria stands as a symbol of faith, history, and architectural beauty. Its origins trace back to the 18th century when it was founded by monks seeking refuge from pirate raids and invasions. Over the years, the monastery has played a vital role in the island's history and spiritual life, making it a significant landmark for both locals and visitors.

As holidaymakers approach the monastery, they'll be greeted by its elegant stone façade, adorned with intricate carvings and traditional architectural elements. The complex comprises various buildings, courtyards, and chapels, each reflecting a blend of Byzantine, Venetian, and Greek influences that have shaped the island's cultural tapestry.

Upon entering the monastery grounds, visitors will experience a sense of serenity and tranquility. The well-maintained gardens, fragrant flowers, and peaceful atmosphere create an ideal setting for reflection and contemplation. Families on vacation can explore the site together, sharing in its historical and spiritual significance.

Inside the monastery, holidaymakers can discover ornate frescoes, religious icons, and artifacts that provide insights into the religious practices and cultural heritage of Skiathos. The main church, dedicated to the Annunciation of the Virgin Mary, is a masterpiece of architecture and artistry, offering a glimpse into the island's devotion and artistic legacy.

For those interested in history, the Monastery of Evangelistria also houses a museum where visitors can learn about the monastery's history, its role in the Greek War of Independence, and the contributions of its monks to the island's development.

Biotope

For holidaymakers seeking to connect with the natural beauty and biodiversity of Skiathos, a visit to the Biotope is a unique and enriching experience that offers a glimpse into the island's delicate ecosystems and wildlife.

The Biotope, also known as the Strofilia Lake, is a natural wetland area that serves as a haven for various plant and animal species. Located on the southwestern side of Skiathos, this protected natural reserve offers a stark contrast to the island's beaches and towns, allowing visitors to immerse themselves in a serene and untouched environment.

As holidaymakers approach the Biotope, they'll be greeted by a tranquil landscape that includes reed beds, shallow waters, and lush vegetation. The area's significance lies in its role as a stopping point for migratory birds, making it an ideal destination for birdwatching enthusiasts and nature lovers.

The diversity of bird species that visit the Biotope throughout the year is astounding. From graceful herons and colorful kingfishers to secretive warblers and majestic birds of prey, the area provides a remarkable opportunity to observe these creatures in their natural habitat. Binoculars and cameras are highly recommended for capturing the beauty of these avian residents.

For families on vacation, the Biotope offers an educational experience that introduces children to the wonders of nature and the importance of conservation. Children can learn about the various bird species, wetland ecosystems, and the fragile balance that sustains life in this unique environment.

Walking paths and observation points allow visitors to explore the Biotope while minimizing disruption to its delicate ecosystem. It's important to follow any guidelines or recommendations provided by local authorities to ensure a respectful visit that contributes to the preservation of the area.

While exploring the Biotope, holidaymakers will also have the chance to encounter other inhabitants of the wetland, such as turtles, frogs, and various aquatic plants. The scenery provides a welcome respite from the bustling tourist areas and a chance to reconnect with nature in a tranquil setting.

House of Papadiamantis

For holidaymakers looking to delve into the literary heritage of Skiathos and gain insights into the life and work of a prominent Greek writer, a visit to the House of Papadiamantis is a must. This historic site provides a window into the world of Alexandros Papadiamantis, a celebrated author whose works have left a lasting impact on Greek literature.

Located in the heart of Skiathos town, the House of Papadiamantis stands as a tribute to the writer's legacy and offers a unique opportunity to step back in time. As holidaymakers approach the house, they'll be greeted by a charming traditional building adorned with architectural elements typical of the era in which Papadiamantis lived.

Once inside, visitors will find themselves immersed in a world that blends history, literature, and cultural heritage. The rooms have been meticulously preserved to reflect the lifestyle of the late 19th and early 20th centuries, giving holidaymakers a glimpse into the everyday life of the author and the island's inhabitants during that era.

The house is furnished with period-appropriate items, including furniture, household items, and personal belongings that belonged to Papadiamantis and his family. This immersive experience allows visitors to connect with the writer's surroundings and gain a deeper understanding of the context in which his literary masterpieces were created.

Throughout the house, informative displays, exhibits, and photographs provide insights into Papadiamantis' life, his contributions to Greek literature, and the historical backdrop against which he wrote. Families on vacation can explore the house together, making it an educational and engaging experience for children and adults alike.

For literature enthusiasts, the House of Papadiamantis serves as a tribute to the writer's creativity and enduring impact on Greek culture. Visitors can gain insights into his creative process, his inspirations, and the themes that permeate his works.

Monastery of Panagia Kounistra

Situated amidst the lush pine forests of Skiathos, the Monastery of Panagia Kounistra, also known as the Monastery of Our Lady of Kounistra, holds a special place in the hearts of locals and visitors alike. As holidaymakers approach the monastery, they'll be captivated by the harmonious blend of natural beauty and architectural grace that defines the site.

The monastery's origins can be traced back to the late 17th century, making it a repository of centuries-old religious and cultural history. Its distinct location, nestled amidst the verdant landscape, adds to the atmosphere of peaceful contemplation that surrounds the site.

Upon entering the monastery grounds, visitors are welcomed by an ambiance of tranquility and spirituality.

The main church, dedicated to the Virgin Mary, boasts an impressive façade adorned with intricate carvings and religious symbols. Inside, ornate frescoes, icons, and religious artifacts contribute to the aura of reverence and devotion.

Families on vacation can explore the various buildings, chapels, and courtyards that make up the monastery complex. Children can learn about the history and significance of the monastery while absorbing the peaceful surroundings that make it a unique destination.

One of the highlights of the Monastery of Panagia Kounistra is its panoramic views of the island's landscape. The monastery's elevated position offers holidaymakers breathtaking vistas of Skiathos' coastline, azure waters, and lush forests. This makes it an ideal spot for capturing memorable photographs and embracing the island's natural beauty.

A visit to the monastery is also an opportunity to observe local traditions and rituals. Depending on the time of year, visitors may have the chance to witness religious ceremonies, festivals, or special events that provide insights into the island's cultural heritage.

Church of Three Bishops

The Church of Three Bishops, also known as Agios Nikolaos, is a prominent religious site located in the heart of Skiathos town. As holidaymakers approach the church, they'll be greeted by its traditional white façade adorned with intricate architectural details that reflect the island's distinctive style.

Upon entering the church, visitors will be struck by the serene and contemplative atmosphere that envelops the interior. The church's interior is adorned with religious icons, ornate frescoes, and exquisite woodwork that showcases the craftsmanship of a bygone era. The flickering candlelight and the scent of incense create an ambiance of reverence and devotion.

The church is dedicated to three bishops who were instrumental in spreading Christianity in the region: Saint Athanasius, Saint Nicholas, and Saint Simeon. The presence of these revered figures adds a layer of historical and spiritual significance to the site.

Holidaymakers can take a moment to offer their respects, light a candle, or simply soak in the sense of tranquility that pervades the Church of Three Bishops. Families on vacation can also use this opportunity to educate their children about the importance of religious heritage and cultural traditions.

One of the most enchanting aspects of the Church of Three Bishops is its central location within Skiathos town. As visitors explore the surrounding streets, they can easily stumble upon this gem of a church, which serves as a focal point for both locals and tourists.

The church's role in local life extends beyond its spiritual function. Throughout the year, it hosts religious ceremonies, festivals, and events that offer insights into the island's cultural traditions. Depending on the timing of your visit, you might have the chance to witness a special occasion that adds an extra layer of authenticity to your experience.

When visiting religious sites like the Church of Three Bishops, it's important to dress modestly and adhere to any guidelines provided by the local authorities. This ensures a respectful and meaningful visit that honors both the site's spiritual significance and the island's cultural heritage.

Church of Agios Nikolaos

The Church of Agios Nikolaos, also known as the Church of Saint Nicholas, is a prominent religious edifice located in the heart of Skiathos town. As visitors approach the church, they are greeted by its distinctive white façade adorned with intricate architectural details that reflect the island's unique aesthetic.

Upon entering the church, holidaymakers will be enveloped by an atmosphere of tranquility and devotion. The interior of the church is adorned with exquisite religious icons, intricate frescoes, and ornate woodwork that exemplify the craftsmanship of the past. The interplay of soft candlelight and the aroma of incense create a sense of reverence and introspection.

This church is dedicated to Saint Nicholas, a revered figure in Christianity known for his compassion and generosity. The presence of Saint Nicholas adds a layer of historical and spiritual significance to the site, drawing pilgrims and travelers alike to seek solace and connection.

The Church of Agios Nikolaos provides a space for reflection, prayer, and contemplation. Visitors may choose to light a candle, offer their respects, or simply bask in the serene ambiance that emanates from the heart of the church. Families on vacation can also seize the opportunity to educate their children about the importance of religious heritage and the island's cultural traditions.

What makes the Church of Agios Nikolaos particularly enchanting is its central location within Skiathos town. As visitors explore the charming streets and alleys, they can easily stumble upon this hidden gem of a church, which serves as a touchstone for both locals and tourists alike.

Beyond its role as a spiritual sanctuary, the church plays a part in the island's cultural life. Throughout the year, the church hosts a variety of religious ceremonies, festivals, and events that offer insights into the island's rich traditions. Depending on the timing of your visit, you might have the chance to witness a special occasion that deepens your connection to the local culture.

SOME OFF-THE-BEATEN-PATH LOCATIONS IN SKIATHOS

Kounistra Monastery Gardens: Surrounding the Monastery of Panagia Kounistra, these gardens offer a peaceful refuge filled with vibrant flowers, aromatic herbs, and serene pathways. The gardens invite visitors to stroll and reflect amidst nature's beauty.

Megali Ammos Hill: Hike to the top of Megali Ammos Hill for a panoramic view that captures the island's coastline in all its splendor. This vantage point offers a breathtaking vista that's especially enchanting during sunset.

Achladia Village: Nestled amid pine-covered hills, Achladia Village provides a tranquil escape. Stroll through the village's narrow streets, admire the traditional architecture, and savor the quiet charm of a less-visited corner of Skiathos.

Diamandi Bay: Hidden away from the more crowded beaches, Diamandi Bay is a small paradise with calm waters and a peaceful atmosphere. Whether you're sunbathing or snorkeling, this secret gem offers a slice of paradise.

Koukounaries Peninsula: Escape the crowds by hiking to the Koukounaries Peninsula. This lesser-visited area boasts secluded coves, breathtaking views, and an intimate connection with nature.

Arkos Island: Venture beyond Skiathos to the uninhabited Arkos Island. A boat trip takes you to this untouched paradise, where you can snorkel, swim, and bask in the seclusion of nature.

Kastro Rock Pools: Embark on a rewarding hike to discover the natural rock pools near Kastro. These hidden pools offer a unique and refreshing spot to cool off while surrounded by nature's beauty.

Galaria Forest: Step into the heart of nature by exploring the Galaria Forest. This lesser-known area offers hiking trails, lush greenery, and a peaceful environment for those seeking a deeper connection with Skiathos' landscapes.

NEARBY DAY TRIPS FROM SKIATHOS

Skopelos Island

You might recognize Skopelos Island as one of the filming locations for Mamma Mia. If you thought Skiathos was lush, wait until you experience this destination. Situated to the east of Skiathos and accessible by an 80-minute boat journey, over fifty percent of the island is covered by untouched pine forests.

Additionally, olive and almond trees flourish here, and the island is known for producing locally sourced honey. Exploring the main town, you'll encounter a delightful blend of charming tavernas and bars.

For those seeking relaxation, Skopelos Island boasts a coastline of approximately 70 kilometers (43 miles), featuring beaches adorned with trees, pebbles, and sand. Notably, Kastani Beach, which was also featured in Mamma Mia, is among these inviting coastal spots.

Punta Peninsula

Featuring a captivating array of golden beaches, evergreen pine forests, and serene olive groves, the Punta Peninsula is a truly idyllic destination that merits inclusion in your Skiathos sailing itinerary. The advantage is that the Punta Peninsula is just a brief sail away from Skiathos Town, conveniently close to the airport.

Dropping anchor at the breathtakingly windswept Lazareta Beach offers the perfect opportunity for a leisurely day of sunbathing and swimming. You can replenish your energy with Greek snacks on board, ensuring you're ready for more activities.

Tsougria Island

Position yourself under the clock tower in Skiathos Town and you'll have an unobstructed view of Tsougria Island. This outcrop is just a short boat ride away, with the cruise costing approximately €10 if you're without your own vessel. Regular cruises make stops at Tsougria Island. Once there, you can indulge in sunbathing on any of the island's four sandy beaches or embark on a hike up the rugged ridge, which rewards you with panoramic vistas of Skiathos and neighboring Skopelos.

While Tsougria remains uninhabited, a stylish beach bar typically operates on the northwest coast during the summer months.

Lalaria Beach

The stunning Lalaria Beach is exclusively accessible by boat from the port at Skiathos Town and is located on the northeastern tip of the island. Anticipate a broad expanse of sugary sand framed by towering white cliffs. The standout feature of this location is the natural rock bridge that stretches across the sand and arches gracefully over the exceptionally clear sea.

The remarkable "blue" and "black" caves are situated just before Lalaria Beach and certainly warrant a visit. It's important to note that there are no beach bars along this stretch, so make sure to bring your refreshments ashore.

Alonissos Island:

Alonissos is perfect for a more tranquil experience. The Old Village (Chora) is a delight to explore with its narrow alleys, traditional houses, and stunning sea views.

The island's marine park is a haven for wildlife enthusiasts and offers the chance to spot rare and endangered species. For a relaxing day, you can unwind on beautiful beaches like Agios Dimitrios or Kokkinokastro.

Pelion Peninsula:

The Pelion Peninsula combines mountainous landscapes with picturesque villages and gorgeous beaches. Tsagarada is known for its stunning architecture and vibrant natural surroundings, while Portaria offers a more traditional atmosphere with cobblestone streets and stone houses.

Milopotamos Beach is famous for its natural rock formations and the crystal-clear "Fakistra" beach is accessible via a beautiful hiking trail.

Evia Island:

Evia offers a diverse range of experiences. The town of Edipsos is famous for its thermal springs and therapeutic baths. In the mountain village of Dimitsana, you can explore stone-built houses, picturesque bridges, and the Liarimma Gorge. Relax on the beaches of Limnionas or explore the ancient ruins of Eretria.

OUTDOOR ACTIVITIES IN SKIATHOS

If you're seeking adventure and excitement during your island getaway, Skiathos offers a diverse range of thrilling activities for an energetic vacation.

Sailing

Sailing is a highly popular pursuit on Skiathos due to the favorable conditions of the waters and wind. You can find various sailing boats available for rent at Skiathos Town's port and well-known beaches. These boats provide a great way to explore the island's splendid secluded shores like Lygaries while enjoying the crystal-clear sea. Novice sailors might prefer the smoother conditions of the southern part of the island.

Additionally, organized daily sailing trips and yacht excursions are offered, venturing to otherwise inaccessible beaches and nearby islands such as Skopelos and Alonissos. This presents an excellent opportunity to explore the surroundings of Skiathos while unwinding. Most sailing cruises operate between April and October.

Trekking

For those who adore nature and trekking, Skiathos can be a paradise with its 24 well-marked hiking trails. These trails take you through unspoiled landscapes of remarkable beauty, along with historical sites.

You have a wide array of trekking options catering to different interests. Whether you're up for adventurous walks, wine tasting or medicinal herb discovery, Skiathos has it all. The trails lead from one secluded beach to another, as well as to impressive monasteries, old chapels, and enchanting fountains.

The best months for trekking in Skiathos are April, May, September, and October due to the more moderate temperatures. Guided walks are also available, with popular routes including the path from Skiathos Town to the Evangelistria Monastery and the Castle, as well as the route from Megali Ammos Beach to the Kehria Monastery.

Water Sports

The protected southern coast of the island is a haven for water sports enthusiasts. This is one of the top activities in Skiathos. Many of the well-known southern beaches offer water sports centers. Megali Ammos stands out as the most excellently equipped beach, boasting numerous facilities for enjoyable games. Following closely are beaches like Koukounaries, Kanapitsa, Ahladies, Agia Eleni, and Vromolimnos.

You'll find an extensive selection of exciting water sports, including water skiing, wakeboarding, ski boat or banana slide rides, and jet skiing. On-site water sports lessons and equipment rental make it easy for everyone to participate.

Beach Fun:

Skiathos is all about beaches! You can relax on the soft sand, swim in the clear blue water, and even try some snorkeling to see the fish and colorful underwater world. Some popular beaches to visit are Koukounaries, Banana Beach, and Lalaria Beach.

Hiking Adventures:

If you like exploring on foot, there are hiking trails that take you through forests and up hills for amazing views. One popular trail goes to Kastro, an old fortress with a fantastic lookout over the sea.

Biking Around:

Hire a bicycle and cycle around the island. You'll find quiet roads and paths that lead you to charming villages, beautiful beaches, and lovely countryside views.

Sunset Watching:

Don't miss the stunning sunsets in Skiathos. Find a nice spot by the sea, maybe even on a boat, and watch as the sky turns all shades of orange, pink, and purple. It's a enchanting method to conclude your day.

Exploring Old Town:

Skiathos Town is really charming. You can stroll through its narrow streets, discover little shops, and grab a bite to eat at a local taverna. The town is especially lovely in the evening when the lights come on.

Bird-Watching: If you're into nature, you might enjoy bird-watching on the island. Skiathos is home to a variety of bird species, so bring your binoculars and see what you can spot!

Photography: If you're into taking pictures, Skiathos is a photographer's dream. Capture the stunning beaches, the clear waters, and the charming architecture around the island.

Remember to wear sunscreen, stay hydrated, and have fun while enjoying all these outdoor activities on the beautiful island of Skiathos!

A PERFECT SEVEN-DAY ITINERARY FOR A VISIT TO SKIATHOS

Here's a suggested itinerary that combines relaxation, exploration, and enjoying the island's natural beauty:

Day 1: Arrival and Beach Time

Arrive in Skiathos and check in to your accommodation.

Head to Koukounaries Beach, one of the most famous on the island. Relax on the soft sand and take a refreshing swim in the clear blue waters.

In the evening, explore Skiathos Town's old port area, enjoy a delicious Greek dinner at a waterfront taverna, and take in the charming atmosphere.

Day 2: Sailing Adventure

Start the day with a sailing adventure. Join a boat tour that takes you around the island, exploring hidden coves and caves.

Enjoy a swim in the crystal-clear waters and indulge in a beach picnic provided by the tour.

Return to Skiathos Town in the late afternoon and unwind at a beachside cafe.

Day 3: Trekking and Exploration

Embark on a morning trekking adventure. Choose a trail that takes you through forests and offers panoramic views. The trail to Kastro is a great option.

After your trek, visit the Evangelistria Monastery and learn about its history.

Spend the afternoon relaxing at Megali Ammos Beach, enjoying water sports, or simply soaking up the sun.

Day 4: Day Trip to Skopelos

Take a ferry to Skopelos Island for a day trip. Explore the charming town, visit the Agios Ioannis church (famous from "Mamma Mia!"), and enjoy a lunchtime meal at a tavern close by.

Relax on one of Skopelos' beautiful beaches or go for a swim in the clear waters.

Return to Skiathos in the evening.

Day 5: Water Sports and Evening Stroll

Spend the morning indulging in water sports at one of the southern beaches like Koukounaries or Megali Ammos.

In the afternoon, explore the charming streets of Skiathos Town, shop for souvenirs, and enjoy an evening stroll along the old port.

Day 6: Relaxation and Sunset Watching

Dedicate the day to relaxation. Choose a tranquil beach like Banana Beach or Lalaria Beach for a peaceful day of swimming and sunbathing.

In the evening, head to a scenic spot to watch the stunning sunset over the sea.

Day 7: Biking and Farewell

Rent a bike and explore the island's countryside. Ride through picturesque villages and stop at viewpoints for breathtaking photos.

Return to Skiathos Town and spend your last afternoon shopping for local products and enjoying a final Greek meal.

Depart from Skiathos with wonderful memories of your island adventure.

Remember that this itinerary is just a suggestion, and you can adjust it based on your preferences and the activities you enjoy most. Skiathos offers a perfect mix of relaxation, outdoor activities, and cultural experiences, ensuring you have an unforgettable 7-day vacation!

CULTURAL FESTIVALS AND HOLIDAYS

The local celebrations held in Skiathos are accompanied by traditional cuisine, live musical performances, and an abundance of wine, welcoming both island residents and tourists alike. These festivities underscore the significance of heritage and age-old traditions, as demonstrated by the island's various local fairs and revelries.

Agios Georgios Festival:

Every April 23rd (or the Monday following Easter if April 23rd falls within Holy Week), Skiathos honors the feast of Agios Georgios with grand festivities. On this occasion, horse races are organized, followed by an open panigiri, where locals present delectable dishes and engage in the traditional Kamara dance.

July 25th Celebration:

On the 25th of July, a substantial celebration takes place to commemorate the feast of Agia Paraskevi. This festive event involves dance, culinary delights, and beverages. The panigiri commences after the evening litany of the icon, paraded through the streets of Skiathos Town.

March 25th Event:

Marking March 25th, a commemoration occurs at the Monastery of Panagia Evangelistria, situated at the heart of the island.

Katsonia Festival:

The Katsonia Festival is observed in September on Skiathos Island, serving as a tribute to the Greek submarine "Lambros Katsonis," which met its fate near Skiathos in September 1943, during the Second World War. Locals participate by tossing flowers into the Aegean Sea.

Bourtzi Festival:

Throughout the summer season, a diverse range of cultural events unfolds at Bourtzi, the ancient fortress nestled between Skiathos Island's old and new ports. The schedule encompasses theatrical presentations, art exhibitions, musical concerts, film screenings, and even performances of Greek shadow theater (Karagiozis).

Zoodoxhos Phgh Celebration:

The country church of Zoodoxhos Phgh, located 7 kilometers northwest of Skiathos Town, was established following the discovery of an icon of Panagia atop a fountain. Annually, on the first Friday after Easter, locals commemorate the unearthing of the "Fountain of Life" (Zoodoxhos Pighi) with customary songs and dances.

August 15th Observance:

On August 15th, the Evagelistria Monastery observes the Ascension of the Virgin Mary through a poignant epitaphios service, uniting local residents in celebration. This unique epitaphios procession, a rarity in Greece, draws Greeks from urban areas to islands and villages for the festivities.

November 21st - Kounistra Festival:

On November 21st, the Kounistra Monastery marks the Presentation of the Virgin Mary. On November 20th, the original Virgin Mary icon housed in the "Trion Ierarchon" church is transported by foot to the Kounistra monastery via a mountain route. An artillery salute is offered en route, honoring the icon's departure from Acropolis (near bus stop no. 4). Throughout the night, prayers are offered at the monastery, and at dawn, the icon returns to the town church.

Agia Paraskevi Celebration:

July 26th witnesses the Agia Paraskevi Feast, providing a splendid opportunity to witness the island's vibrant folk dances. Visitors are encouraged to participate. The day is enhanced by traditional music and captivating local attire, creating an immensely enjoyable ambiance. Situated across from the Magic Hotel, we heartily recommend our guests to visit the church during this special occasion.

Carnival (Apokries):

Skiathos celebrates Carnival with lively festivities leading up to Lent. Colorful parades, masked dances, and traditional music fill the streets. Locals and visitors alike join in the fun, wearing costumes and enjoying the festive atmosphere.

Easter:

Easter is a significant holiday in Greece, and Skiathos observes it with religious processions, church services, and a strong sense of community. The Good Friday evening procession, where people carry an epitaph (a symbolic representation of Christ's tomb), is a moving experience. On Easter Sunday, enjoy a festive meal with traditional dishes and red-dyed eggs.

Festival of Agios Riginos:

Celebrated on February 25th, this festival honors Agios Riginos, the island's patron saint. A religious procession takes place, with the icon of the saint paraded through the streets of Skiathos Town. The celebration reflects the island's deep religious roots.

Festival of Agios Fanourios:

On August 27th, the island celebrates Agios Fanourios, the patron saint of lost things. This festival involves church services, processions, and a joyful atmosphere, as people come together to honor the saint and seek his blessings.

Independence Day (March 25th):

A nationwide holiday in Greece, Skiathos commemorates Independence Day with a parade and celebrations. School children, military personnel, and local organizations march through the streets of Skiathos Town, showcasing patriotism and national pride.

International Papadiamantis Festival:

Dedicated to the famous Greek writer Alexandros Papadiamantis, this festival takes place in early September. It includes literary events, exhibitions, performances, and discussions that celebrate Greek literature, culture, and the island's literary heritage.

Wine Festival:

In September, Skiathos hosts a wine festival celebrating local wines and traditional Greek music and dance. It's a great opportunity to savor local flavors, learn about winemaking, and enjoy the lively atmosphere.

Saint John's Day (Ioannis Prodromos):

Celebrated on June 24th, this religious holiday includes church services and often involves outdoor gatherings with food, music, and dance. It's a wonderful occasion to experience local customs and hospitality.

BEST BEACHES IN SKIATHOS

Renowned for their verdant backdrop of pine and olive trees, shimmering blue-green waters, and the delightful mix of fine sand and pebbles, the beaches of Skiathos gleam like fragments of sun-kissed Greek treasure.

A remarkable ten of these beaches have been honored with Blue Flags for their environmental cleanliness. These coastal havens span the spectrum from fully equipped, featuring tavernas, beach bars, and water sports facilities, to the blissfully secluded.

So, whether you've already secured your upcoming vacation to Skiathos or are seeking inspiration on where to venture, there's only one element that's yet to grace your experience: a checklist of Skiathos' must-visit beaches.

Lalaria Beach:

Lalaria Beach promises to etch a lasting imprint in your memory. Earning the distinction of being one of Skiathos' most renowned beaches (though Koukounaries might engage in a friendly debate), Lalaria's allure is as crystal-clear as its profound azure waters. This ethereal haven is accessible solely by boat, boasting its distinct identity through its smooth, ivory pebbles and the towering white cliffs that stand sentinel over sunbathers.

An Instagram-worthy moment awaits at one end, where a sizable hole in the rock (known as Tripia Petra or Perforated Stone) extends into the sea. The rugged coastline creates an ideal backdrop for snorkeling, and the neighboring sea caves often feature in boat excursions.

Koukounaries Beach:

Another crown jewel on any compilation of Skiathos' premier beaches, the Blue Flag-adorned Koukounaries epitomizes the embrace of a cozy blanket during Greek getaways.

The encompassing pine grove, which flanks the entirety of the beach, melds seamlessly with the translucent emerald-blue waters, a seduction capable of captivating all who tread upon this haven. Embrace the horizontal life with a good book or explore the Natura 2000-protected Lake Strofylia that lies adjacent to the beach, a sanctuary for migratory bird species.

The verdant carpet of surroundings seamlessly merges with the cosmopolitan ambiance of Koukounaries Beach, tempting visitors to linger until the hues of sunset merge with evening cocktails.

Megalos & Mikros Aselinos Beaches:

Megalos and Mikros Aselinos, twin beauties gracing Skiathos' shoreline, rest side by side, their backdrop of lush greenery harmonizing with the azure waters and alabaster pebbled sands. Megalos Aselinos offers slightly more amenities, including a taverna, while Mikros Aselinos, with fewer visitors, exude tranquility.

Both beaches feature a lively breeze and deep waters, catering well to water enthusiasts equipped with flippers and goggles.

Vromolimnos Beach:

Radiating vibrant energy, Vromolimnos stands out among Skiathos' liveliest beaches. Nestled within a serene cove, its soft golden sands and verdant fringes extend gracefully into the sea.

A tropical aura envelops this beach, encouraging carefree splashing and basking under the sun's embrace. Rent water sports equipment for stand-up paddleboarding, water skiing, wakeboarding, or jet skiing. Consider embarking on a boat adventure to explore the nearby shores or delight in beach bars and tavernas at Kolios Beach.

Troulos Beach:

Set amid a verdant canopy, Troulos' sandy paradise beckons families with its Blue Flag distinction, shallow turquoise waters, and choice of sunbeds, umbrellas, or the natural shade provided by trees.

Among Skiathos' most tranquil beaches, Troulos exudes a relaxed and unpretentious atmosphere. The graceful swans that occasionally grace the beach further enhance the serene ambiance.

Elia Beach:

Tucked away in the untamed northern realm of the island, Elia resides within a serene palm-fringed bay, secluded and ideal for rejuvenation. This idyllic expanse offers ample facilities, with its green-blue shallows making it an inviting destination for families and relaxation seekers.

Sunset enthusiasts will be captivated by the beach's twilight allure. Nearby Mandraki Beach, a natural wonder, beckons as a delightful neighbor.

Krifi Ammos Beach:

Secluded and untamed, Krifi Ammos stands as another of Skiathos' Instagram-worthy treasures. Nestled within a U-shaped cove embellished with lush trees, this exquisite sandy stretch gradually slopes into inviting green-blue waters, creating an excellent venue for snorkeling.

Despite its popularity, arriving early is recommended to secure a prime spot on this scenic gem.

Xanemos Beach:

Xanemos Beach presents an intriguing blend of two unexpected elements in a Skiathos vacation: horseback riding (booking in advance is advisable) and witnessing legendary airplane landings at the neighboring airport. Amidst these thrills, the beach's atmosphere remains tranquil and unspoiled, characterized by sandy pebbles that kiss the clear, deep waters.

Located conveniently near Skiathos Town, it's a perfect destination for splitting your day between different activities.

Kastro Beach:

Graced by clear blue waters and surrounded by verdure, Kastro Beach rests below Skiathos' medieval town and its Byzantine castle, in perfect harmony with its namesake. For those exploring the fortress, this beach proves an excellent complement. Access involves a short but steep descent or, alternately, Kastro Beach serves as a highlight on various boat trips to Lalaria Beach.

Don't forget to bring your snorkeling gear to explore the captivating underwater world.

Ligaries Beach:

Nestled within a charming green bay, Ligaries claims a spot among Skiathos' most picturesque shores. While reaching this treasure requires navigating a dirt road, the reward is a beach brimming with character. White sands, green-blue waters, and breathtaking sunsets all contribute to Ligaries' allure.

A detour to neighboring Kechria Beach, renowned for its photogenic rock and seaside taverna, is a recommended addition to your itinerary.

SKIATHOS FOR FAMILIES

Family-Friendly Activities and Experiences

Skiathos, with its plethora of beaches, emerges as an ideal family destination. Yet, the island offers far more to explore. During your visit, a diverse range of activities and attractions awaits, tailored to suit your family's interests. Here's a glimpse of what you can look forward to when embarking on a family adventure to Skiathos, Greece.

Embark on Exciting Adventures in Skiathos

The natural beauty and enchanting landscapes that grace Skiathos are nothing short of a blessing. The most authentic way to immerse in this facet of the island is by experiencing it firsthand.

For families with a penchant for the outdoors, bike riding across Skiathos' terrain proves to be an exhilarating choice. Alternatively, meandering on foot is a delightful option, with signposted walking trails guiding you through the unspoiled corners of the island.

Beyond hiking, Skiathos boasts a well-organized horse-riding center, providing an excellent opportunity for those who love horseback exploration. This presents a remarkable means to traverse Skiathos' coastline and picturesque expanses.

Furthermore, Skiathos hosts an array of annual events, enriching your family's stay with vibrant festivities.

Indulge in Skiathos' Culinary Delights

Delighting your taste buds, Skiathos beckons your family to savor its local delicacies. A culinary journey here encompasses specialties like kakavia, a nourishing fish soup; the traditional combination of crawfish and cabbage; octopus paired with fava; the locally cherished cheese pie; and amigdalota, a delectable regional pastry. Skiathos also takes pride in its olive oil, wine, and artisanal pasta.

Amid the island's expanse, you'll encounter tavernas and restaurants serving a medley of Greek and Mediterranean cuisine, along with sumptuous seafood offerings. Alongside these, coffee shops, bakeries, and pastry outlets dot the island, ready to rejuvenate you during your daily escapades.

Family-Friendly Shorelines

Blessed with a remarkable 60 beaches, a majority of which adorn the island's southern stretch, Skiathos stands as a haven for swimming enthusiasts.

Most of these beaches boast soft sand and are well-equipped with sunbeds and umbrellas. While the beaches on the island's northern side offer seclusion and often cater to naturists.

Koukounaries Beach emerges as a pinnacle of beauty and family appeal on Skiathos. Its golden sands and clear, shallow waters create an idyllic setting for children. Arriving early secures a sunbed, as the beach tends to get busier later in the day.

Skiathos' other stunning beaches include Lalaria Beach, Troulos Bay Beach, Big (and Small) Banana Beach, Elia Beach (or Mandraki Beach), Diamandi Beach, and Kastro Beach.

Many organized beaches also host water sports centers, providing avenues for thrilling water activities such as water skiing and banana slides, contributing to unforgettable family moments.

Embarking on Island Voyages

As previously mentioned, Skiathos opens the gateway to island explorations, with boat trips extending to destinations like Skopelos and Alonissos.

Both islands offer a wealth of family-friendly activities, enabling you to explore at a comfortable pace.

Booking separate excursions to experience a day on each island proves a wise choice, ensuring an unhurried and enriching adventure.

Seamless Beach and Island Exploration with Water Taxis

Beyond conventional modes of transportation, Skiathos offers a range of options to traverse its landscape. If you intend to explore the island's seafront, villages, and hidden beaches, consider renting a car, with the option of a 4x4 lending an adventurous touch to your family's journey, uncovering secret coves and mountains.

For those disinclined towards buses or cars, Skiathos offers an uncommon alternative: water taxis.

Water taxis emerge as the epitome of efficiency for beach hopping and navigating the islands' diverse regions. These aquatic vessels provide swift access from your hotel to various locales within Skiathos or even to neighboring islands such as Skopelos and Alonissos.

SKIATHOS FOR COUPLES

Skiathos stands as a haven of romance, evident in the multitude of weddings and honeymoons that grace its shores, reaching their zenith in August each year. The island's allure extends to encompass everything that newlyweds seek in a honeymoon: secluded beaches, luxurious hotels, exquisite dining options, and an abundance of romantic settings to bask in the beauty of sunsets. It is indeed the ultimate destination for couples, offering an enchanting experience without straining the budget.

Here's our guide to crafting a romantic escapade in Skiathos!

Indulge in Welcome Drinks at Bourtzi

Elevate the beginning of your married life and set the tone for your Skiathos sojourn with a leisurely libation at Bourtzi. Nestled on a small peninsula extending into the sea between Skiathos Town's old and new ports, Bourtzi, a historic fortress dating back to the 13th century, boasts a storied past of repelling adversaries and pirate raids. Today, it hosts one of the town's finest bars. Offering a selection of exceptional cocktails and delectable nibbles, the establishment also affords unparalleled airplane spotting opportunities and breathtaking sea vistas.

Don't forget to capture a moment in the restroom, where mirrors are replaced with boundless ocean views – a characteristic that visitors fondly embrace.

Agios Nikolaos Church and Clock Tower

As the sun begins its descent, a visit to Agios Nikolaos Church emerges as one of the quintessential experiences in Skiathos. Scaling approximately 100 steps through ancient alleyways adorned with fragrant jasmine gardens and occasional stone-built bars cocooned in bougainvillea-draped walls, the journey is nothing short of rewarding.

At the summit, panoramic vistas of the town, both new and old ports, unfold, bestowing a magical ambiance ideal for couples.

Delight in a Romantic Dinner at Scuna Restaurant

Savor an intimate evening by the seaside at Scuna, a dining destination exuding romance. Following a day of exploration, including a tour of the northern beaches of Skiathos, we arrived at Scuna on our second night on the island, our appetites whetted and anticipation high.

The restaurant did not disappoint; every dish bore the chef's artistry, while the ambiance reverberated with authentic Greek aromas, accentuated by dried oregano bouquets suspended from the ceiling and an array of Greek wine bottles on display.

Stroll Along the Port

Skiathos boasts a lengthy port, divided into three distinct sections: the old port, the Municipal Port, and the Paraliakos port, which offers the finest vistas of Chora.

Exploration of the old port, nestled adjacent to Bourtzi, invites you to unwind at local bars while observing travelers engage with organizers of island hopping day excursions.

This area also serves as the gateway to booking tickets and embarking on boat journeys to Lalaria Beach, accessible solely by sea.

The Municipal Port serves as the island's principal port, greeting those arriving from the Greek mainland. This hub houses the lifeguard station and is a focal point for the majority of the island's restaurants. It also stands as the departure point for all ferry services, including those to Skopelos.

Last but not least, the Paraliakos Port, an extension of the Municipal Port, curves gracefully, offering spectacular views of the main port and Chora.

Explore Papadiamanti Street

Papadiamantis Alexandros, a celebrated poet hailing from Skiathos, leaves an indelible mark on the island's legacy. His works chronicle the tales of 19th-century life in both rural and urban Greece, weaving narratives of Mediterranean adventures replete with captivity, war, piracy, and illness.

His former residence, now transformed into a museum, graces the main cobbled street of the island, which locals have affectionately named after him as a tribute. Serving as the island's High Street, it offers an array of clothing stores, bars, and souvenir shops. A nighttime excursion along this bustling thoroughfare is an enchanting experience, though daylight hours are ideal for unhurried exploration.

Savor Island Beaches

While Skiathos boasts an array of breathtaking beaches akin to any other Greek island, the most splendid ones grace its northern expanse. These gems, less frequented by visitors, present a serene alternative for those seeking tranquility away from tourist crowds.

For an unhindered beach exploration journey, consider renting a motorbike, especially for accessing beaches that might prove challenging to reach via public transportation or conventional vehicles.

Though Koukounaries is the island's most renowned beach, closely followed by Lalaria Beach, we opted for quieter, lesser-visited havens such as the magnificent Troulos, Kanapitsa, and Krifi Ammos. Imagining a breakfast at Troulos Beach, where a pair of swans elegantly glide through the sea, remains an unforgettable experience.

Visit the Iera Moni Evangelismou tis Theokotou

A visit to this monastery emerges as an imperative when exploring Skiathos. The tranquility and serene vistas of nature that envelop the monastery offer a sense of peace and contentment transcending religious affiliations. A visit during the afternoon, when visitor numbers are lower, affords the opportunity to enjoy the company of monastery cats, eager to guide you through the premises.

SHOPPING AND DINING

Local Cuisines and Specialties

The essence of the wholesome and nourishing Mediterranean diet is well-known, a manifestation that is prominently reflected in Greek cuisine. A melange of delectable vegetables, succulent fruits, and modest amounts of dairy and meat, all harmoniously united by the renowned Greek olive oil.

Yet, beyond this familiarity lies a lesser-known facet: the diverse regional variations that encompass Greek cuisine, where distinctive dishes emerge to represent individual islands or localities. These dishes encapsulate the unique traditions, history, and collective experiences that define the Greek identity.

Skiathos, too, adheres to this culinary phenomenon, boasting a repertoire of remarkable local dishes that has catapulted it into the limelight as a mecca for food enthusiasts and connoisseurs. To assist you in your culinary voyage, we have curated a list of the most celebrated and iconic dishes that Skiathos has to offer, ensuring you embark on a gastronomic adventure like no other!

Kalapodia

Kalapodia, a savory indulgence, showcases hand-kneaded dough artfully infused with local wild greens and herbs. The result is a delectable creation baked to a delightful blend of crispness on the exterior and a warm, creamy interior. These delights serve as a popular local snack or a gratifying breakfast option.

Skiathitiki Tyropita (Skiathos Cheese Pie)

Skiathos cheese pie, revered for its excellence, has left such an indelible mark that it earned praise from not one, but two of Greece's literary luminaries. This masterpiece is meticulously crafted by rolling thin hand-kneaded dough, enclosing a filling of locally sourced soft Greek cheese interwoven with an aromatic medley of herbs.

The symphony of flavors is enriched with eggs and generous quantities of butter, creating a tantalizing spiral of exquisite taste.

Syvrasi with Tomato and Grouper Fish

The culinary technique of "syvrasi" takes center stage in various dishes, commencing with sautéed onions cooked over medium heat, coaxing out their essence and juices. This foundational step paves the way for an ensemble of complementary vegetables. In the case of this emblematic dish, the syvrasi becomes the canvas for a vibrant composition of freshly diced tomato and grouper fish.

The resultant masterpiece orchestrates a symphony of robust flavors that achieve a harmonious equilibrium, culminating in a profoundly gratifying culinary experience.

Crayfish with Wild Greens

Skiathos' history reveals a creative transformation of humble ingredients, as crayfish and similar seafood evolved from their unassuming origins to become cherished delicacies. Embracing this heritage, crayfish is artfully combined with a medley of cooked wild greens, encompassing spinach, chard, chicory, and an array of fragrant herbs. The ensemble dances harmoniously in olive oil, melding their aromas and flavors to accentuate the crayfish's prominence.

Monkfish Stifado

While the renowned stifado, a cherished Greek beef stew, is a familiar entity, Skiathos' interpretation takes a captivating twist, replacing beef with monkfish. Monkfish, a prized catch in Greece, finds itself immersed in a symphony of small onions, tomatoes, generous doses of olive oil, and an array of herbs, including laurel, allspice, rosemary, and oregano. The monkfish's essence is heightened through a gentle infusion in lemon water before joining the stew. A final flourish of wine crowns this culinary masterpiece, resulting in an opulent, must-try delicacy.

Alonissos Tuna with Pasta

Tuna, revered as a local delicacy from Alonissos, a neighboring island within the Sporades archipelago, weaves its magic in a remarkable dish when paired with pasta. The tuna undergoes a transformation in a tomato and sautéed onion stew, heightened by fragrant basil and oregano.

This tantalizing concoction harmoniously melds with pasta, culminating in a truly satisfying culinary encounter.

Kakavia of Skiathos (Traditional Fish Soup)

Kakavia, traditionally denoting a fish soup, takes on a distinct form in Skiathos, where several small fish, encompassing diverse varieties, converge to create a flavorful symphony.

The innovation lies in the technique; instead of being fashioned into a soup, these fish are oven-baked alongside potatoes and abundant onions.

This unique preparation results in an irresistible melding of flavors, epitomizing the island's culinary ingenuity.

Haimalia

An indulgent dessert that encapsulates Skiathos' culinary prowess is Haimalia, a delicacy both irresistible and unique to the island. Deep-fried dough envelops a filling of honey, nuts, cinnamon, and nutmeg, culminating in a symphony of textures and flavors.

This confection, reminiscent of pendants, is named for its pendant-like form, radiating an irresistible allure that once graced weddings and joyous celebrations.

Aspro

A dessert exclusive to Skiathos, Aspro is as rare as it is elusive, typically sourced through local connections.

Traditionally reserved for engagement festivities, this pure white confection derives its name ("aspro," translating to "white" in Greek) from its pristine hue, symbolizing purity.

Crafted from finely chopped, peeled white almonds, it involves a delicate alchemical process, requiring constant whisking to attain the pristine white shade. The result is an exquisite amalgamation of taste and texture that promises an unparalleled gustatory revelation.

Skiathos Baklava

The renowned syrupy delicacy, baklava, which transcends borders and culture, finds a unique expression in Skiathos.

Distinguished by its preparation in a wide, round pan layered with up to 50 wisps of phyllo, this baklava employs almonds, nuts, cinnamon, and copious amounts of butter. This intricate layering bestows a delightful crunch while housing the syrup within, erupting into a symphony of flavors upon each indulgent bite.

Distinctive in its diamond-shaped cut, resembling exquisite embroidery, Skiathos baklava boasts an enchanting visual aesthetic.

With these culinary treasures, Skiathos beckons you to partake in a gastronomic odyssey that encapsulates its rich history, cultural vibrancy, and unparalleled ingenuity.

Popular Restaurants and Cafes

Here is a compilation of our preferred dining establishments within Skiathos Town:

MESOGIA TAVERNA

A family-operated taverna that specializes in uncomplicated, traditional Greek cuisine. Their menu features dishes like grilled meats and fish cooked over a charcoal grill.

Additionally, they offer a selection of vegetarian-friendly options such as saganaki (fried cheese) and kolokithokeftedes (courgette fritters). Our bill, which included two main courses of grilled pork chops and lemon-cooked lamb with potatoes, as well as a €6 half-liter jug of red wine, amounted to a very reasonable €40.

Complimentary choc ices were also generously provided. Please note that reservations are not accepted, so arriving early is recommended.

TO PALOUKI

This vibrant and welcoming eatery, tucked away in the alleys behind the Old Port, consistently draws in patrons night after night. Must-try dishes include drunken pork and the exquisitely tender kleftiko (lamb and potatoes slow-cooked in parchment). With main courses ranging from €10 to €16 and carafes of fine local wine available, the restaurant offers excellent value for money.

1901

An elegant twist on the traditional taverna experience, 1901 boasts a charming ambiance with tables nestled under softly lit trees. Alongside classic Greek fare, the menu includes Italian options like seafood risotto, accompanied by wines from their own vineyard. Reservations are advised, or alternatively, visiting during quieter hours can lead to enjoyable conversations with the staff.

CUCINA DI MARIA

Cucina di Maria is a relaxed Italian restaurant located in Skiathos Town, occupying a cobbled square near the top of the bar steps. The spacious courtyard, shaded by a mulberry tree adorned with vibrant murals, offers a cozy ambiance. The menu focuses on pizzas (including calzones and white pizzas) and pasta dishes like carbonara and arrabiatta. Gluten-free penne is available for most pasta dishes.

With generous portions priced around €14 and a half-liter of local wine for €7.50, this spot is a hit. A complimentary fruit platter is also offered to conclude your meal.

Popular among patrons, be prepared for potential wait times during busy periods, and consider booking ahead for groups larger than two. The leisurely service encourages savoring your meal while people-watching.

GRAVISI

Nestled in the serene streets of Plakes, amidst whitewashed houses adorned with bougainvillea, Gravisi offers a tranquil and picturesque backdrop. Renowned for their Greek-style thin, crispy pizzas, priced at approximately €14, the establishment also provides gluten-free pizza and pasta options upon prior request. Please note that advance notice is recommended to ensure availability.

LO & LA

An Italian-owned gem perched on the steps leading from the Old Port, LO & LA boasts splendid harbor views, especially during twilight. The menu encompasses salads, risottos, and pasta creations like spaghetti ai frutti di mare.

However, it's the exceptionally friendly service that sets it apart, along with complimentary homemade limoncello and dessert.

MARMITA

Magical Marmita beckons with its enchanting setting—a traditional house boasting garden tables nestled amidst trees and flowers adorned with twinkling fairy lights. This establishment is undoubtedly one of the most romantic in Skiathos.

The menu offers an elevated take on traditional Greek cuisine, incorporating seasonal and local ingredients. Dishes range from rabbit cooked in Samos dessert wine to sea bass en papillote, alongside homemade pasta and Greek classics like moussaka and soutzoukakia (baked meatballs).

Mains are priced around €20, representing excellent value for an exceptional meal. Friendly and hospitable staff enhance the experience, with special treats often being presented to patrons. To secure your spot, advance reservations, particularly during the summer months, are essential.

RICCI E POVERA

Positioned above the Old Port, RICCI E POVERA offers a fusion of Mediterranean flavors through its assortment of meat, fish, and vegetable tapas dishes. Lemon-baked cod and samphire with feta and tomato are among their delectable offerings.

With a reasonable price range, five tapas and two glasses of wine can be enjoyed for under €60. Given its cozy size, it's advisable to make reservations in advance, especially if you wish to secure a table with a scenic view.

THE WINDMILL

Situated within a restored windmill from the 1880s, THE WINDMILL boasts some of the most captivating views in town, albeit reached via several steps. A favored spot for romantic sunset dinners, the restaurant presents an international array of dishes, including slow-cooked lamb shank and gremolata-spiced salmon.

The main courses are approximately €25, making it one of the pricier options in Skiathos Town. Advanced booking is essential; however, unusually for Skiathos, online booking is available.

Shopping Districts and Markets

Skiathos Town offers a diverse array of shops catering to a wide range of interests and preferences. The majority of these shops are situated along the bustling main street of the capital, known as Papadiamantis Street.

Within this charming town, visitors can explore a variety of establishments, including stores specializing in local products, footwear boutiques, branded clothing outlets, jewelry stores, art galleries, bookshops, souvenir shops, and gourmet delicacy emporiums. These options provide a delightful spectrum of shopping experiences, allowing visitors to find something that resonates with their tastes.

While it's true that prices in Skiathos Town can be relatively high, taking a leisurely stroll among these diverse shops can be a wonderful way to conclude an evening. The opportunity to admire the splendid array of offerings adds to the allure of the experience, even if one chooses not to make a purchase. Whether it's browsing through local crafts or marveling at exquisite jewelry, Skiathos Town offers a captivating shopping environment that enhances the overall island experience.

Papadiamanti Street:

Named after the famous Greek author Alexandros Papadiamantis, this vibrant street is Skiathos' main shopping hub. Lined with an array of boutiques, galleries, and souvenir shops, Papadiamanti Street is a treasure trove for shoppers. You'll discover everything from traditional Greek handicrafts and artisanal products to clothing, jewelry, and accessories.

Skiathos Town Market:

The central market in Skiathos Town is a lively and bustling place that's worth exploring. Open-air stalls offer a variety of items including fresh produce, local cheeses, spices, and homemade treats. It's a fantastic spot to immerse yourself in the local flavors and fragrances, and perhaps even pick up ingredients for a beach picnic.

Old Port Area:

The picturesque Old Port area is not only a picturesque spot for boat-watching, but it's also home to charming shops that cater to both tourists and locals. You can find an assortment of beachwear, casual clothing, and nautical-inspired accessories. Don't be surprised to stumble upon shops selling seashell jewelry and maritime-themed trinkets.

Traditional Craft Shops:

Venturing through the cobblestone streets, you'll come across traditional craft shops that showcase the island's unique artistry. Look for stores that specialize in pottery, handwoven textiles, and intricate ceramics. These shops offer a glimpse into the island's cultural heritage and make for meaningful keepsakes to take home.

Open-Air Markets:

On certain days, open-air markets set up shop in different parts of the island. These markets are a fantastic opportunity to mingle with locals and discover fresh produce, herbs, handmade crafts, and even vintage items. Keep an eye out for flyers or ask around to find out when and where these markets pop up.

Handmade Jewelry and Art Galleries:

For those with an appreciation for art and craftsmanship, Skiathos boasts a selection of boutiques and galleries that showcase handmade jewelry, paintings, sculptures, and other artistic creations. These pieces often reflect the beauty of the island's natural surroundings.

Beachside Stalls:

As you explore Skiathos' stunning beaches, you'll often find stalls and makeshift shops selling beach essentials like colorful sarongs, sun hats, and local handicrafts. These spots provide a chance to pick up beachwear and accessories while enjoying the sandy shores.

Local Food Markets:

For a true taste of the island's culinary delights, head to local food markets where you can sample and purchase traditional products such as olive oil, honey, herbs, and wines. Engaging with local vendors can also offer insights into the island's food culture and traditions.

Souvenirs and Local Products

In addition to Skiathos' distinctive culinary delights, the island offers a splendid selection of local products to relish. Among the offerings are a diverse range of items such as jams, honey, olive oil, tsipouro (a renowned Greek distilled spirit), premium wines, and liqueurs.

A sought-after souvenir from Skiathos is a bottle of their renowned olive oil, which is prominently produced and cherished on the island. While it might seem commonplace, olive oil is an essential component of Greek cuisine, adorning almost every dish.

Visitors have the opportunity to purchase it in charming souvenir packaging, often in the shape of amphorae or featuring iconic Greek figures. This olive oil can be obtained in 1-liter bottles or in larger 3 or 5-liter jerrycans.

The finest choice is the cold-pressed Extra-Virgin Olive Oil boasting a low acidity level. Following this is Virgin Olive Oil.

For frying, Pure Olive Oil with the addition of refined oil is recommended, although it's not ideal for salad dressings. If opting for oil in a tin container, transferring it to a plastic bottle is advised to preserve its flavor.

However, not all olives are destined for oil production. Local markets showcase an array of fresh olives, each offering a unique flavor profile. A sampling of the various types during your stay is recommended, allowing you to bring back your preferred variety.

The best tinned olives with assorted toppings can be found in local supermarkets, alongside olive paste. With their extended shelf life and affordability, bringing home olives is a tempting option.

Exploring local flavors, don't overlook the opportunity to indulge in local retsina, a Greek wine best served chilled. Local supermarkets stock this refreshing wine in their refrigerators. But do take a moment to peruse the wine shelves, where over seventy varieties of local wine await.

Furthermore, local taverns offer the chance to savor delightful homemade wines. For those seeking stronger libations, anise vodka ouzo, grape vodka grappa, and the local cognac Metaxa are popular options. Don't forget to consider a pack of local coffee as a thoughtful gift.

Olive oil is not confined to culinary use; it's also a fundamental ingredient in natural Greek cosmetics. The rise of natural cosmetics in Greece has been notable in recent years, with handmade olive oil-infused soaps being a hallmark product.

These soaps are available in an array of fragrances, from mint to coffee. Expanding beyond soap, natural shampoos, shower gels, scrubs, and creams can be found. It's advisable to purchase cosmetics from pharmacies or specialized stores to ensure product authenticity and quality, as local markets might not provide the same level of assurance regarding composition.

Komboloi, a well-known Greek accessory, resembles beads strung on a solid thread, typically featuring twenty beads. While not a religious artifact, Komboloi is often used for games and is fashioned from various materials like wood, polymer clay, and even precious or semi-precious stones. Another intriguing option is matopetra, a souvenir associated with superstition, believed to ward off the evil eye.

Skiathos is renowned for its skilled local jewelers who often craft pieces in the Byzantine style. While the island's inhabitants are known for their religious inclination, it's important to note that the icons and religious objects available don't hold historical value.

Keep an eye out for local fur products and intricate lace, but exercise caution in avoiding counterfeit items, which can be found on the market.

NIGHTLIFE IN SKIATHOS

Skiathos Island offers an exhilarating nightlife scene in Skiathos Town, making it an ideal destination for those in search of excitement and vibrancy during their Greek island escapade. In this guide, we will delve into the premier bars and clubs situated in the vicinity, highlighting the best in dancing, cocktails, and panoramic sunset vistas.

It's important to note that Skiathos is a prominent tourist destination, and for the ultimate nightlife encounter, it's advisable to plan your visit between the months of May and September.

Best Bars and Nightclubs

GinFish

Nestled within Skiathos' Old Port, the vibrant outdoor bar known as GinFish offers patrons a breathtaking view of the iconic Byzantine castle, Bourtzi, while indulging them with an assortment of creative cocktails. The lemon pie cocktail stands as a must-try, blending zesty lemon curd with vodka and a hint of cinnamon for a delightful touch of spice. A crushed biscuit rim transforms it into a dessert-like delight.

While cocktails are priced at €12 each, visitors can relish the half-price happy hour from 7-10 pm, making it a definite stop for cocktail enthusiasts.

Address: Old Port On The Waterfront, Skiathos Town, 370 02, Phone: +30 689 247 7702 Website: www.ginfish.gr

Tesla Cocktail Bar

Situated opposite the Papadiamantis House Museum, this steampunk-inspired establishment is a must-visit for those who adore live music. Hosting captivating performances by talented artists covering popular indie tracks, the atmosphere pulses with energy as locals and visitors dance and sing until the early hours of 4 am.

The bar's standout feature is its Tesla's Secret Cocktail Experiments menu, offering a range of characterful concoctions. Sample the Saketini, crafted with sake and locally foraged rock samphire, or opt for CBD-infused cannabis cocktails to keep the night alive.

Address: Mitropolitou Ananiou 12, 370 02 Phone: +30 697 407 8754 Website: www.facebook.com/TESLACOCKTAILBAR

Totem

Adding a unique flair to Skiathos Town's nightlife, Totem is an intimate and distinctive bar that deviates from the typical party scene found in other popular locales. This alternative rock and folk-oriented bar showcases nightly performances by local bands and occasional touring acts from around the world.

The musical spectrum spans from heavy metal guitar riffs to soothing reggae grooves. With seating available indoors and outdoors, Mojave-themed murals adorn the walls, providing a distinct ambiance. The drink menu is wallet-friendly, featuring local ouzo and glasses of prosecco, alongside an impressive cocktail selection.

Apotheke Club

Nestled down Politechniou Street, the renovated warehouse beckons to the younger crowd seeking a trendy and dynamic night out. The expansive space effortlessly transitions from a relaxed hangout into a lively dance-on-the-bar club.

A resident DJ curates a mix of classic Greek pop and international dance tracks, fueling the electric atmosphere. The bar boasts backlit spirit bottles, illuminating the path to a tailor-made cocktail crafted from your preferred mixer.

Address: Skiathos Town, 370 02, Phone: +30 698 761 5959 Website: www.apothekeclub.gr

De Facto

Standing as a prominent LGBTQ+ establishment in Skiathos Town, De Facto is a vibrant and inclusive bar situated just steps away from the harbor. The entrance adorned with rainbow-tinted signage and shimmering fairy lights offers a warm and inviting welcome.

Inside, the bar exudes a small yet lively and colorful ambiance, where Cycladic elements meet disco balls, images of muscular torsos, and neon lights for a captivating blend.

Address: Grigoriou E., Skíathos Phone: +30 698 638 6266 Website: www.facebook.com/DeFactoBarSkiathos

La Bussola

For travelers seeking a unique experience, La Bussola in Koukounaries is a must-visit bar. Their renowned mango margaritas boast a fiery kick of bird's eye chili. The proprietors, Akis and Eleni, are celebrated for their generous pours and genuine warmth. Their extensive knowledge of Skiathos adds a valuable touch to your journey.

Address: Koukounaries 370 02, Phone: +30 697 490 7002 Website: www.facebook.com/labussolabarskiathos

Old Port House Bar

Nestled within a narrow alley off the Skiathos marina, the Old Port House Bar exudes rustic and nautical charm. The interior features timber tables and rough-hewn stone walls painted white, adorned with vintage travel and movie posters.

Local and visitors alike relish the happy hour deals on Mythos draught beer, along with a selection of international brews and rare Guinness IPA on tap. The outdoor seating offers a perfect perch for observing the world pass by on the cobblestone streets.

Address: 28 Nikotsara Street, Skiathos 370 02, Phone: +30 694 566 7883 Website: www.facebook.com/oldporthousebar

ACCOMMODATION OPTIONS

Budget-Friendly Accommodation

Alkyon Lodge Skiathos presents an excellent option for budget-conscious travelers who desire proximity to lively attractions. Situated in the heart of Skiathos Town, it offers a brief stroll to the beach, as well as all the bustling shops and eateries. The establishment features a pool, a bar, and an on-site restaurant. The accommodations are straightforward yet pristine and cozy, with rates ranging from €50 to €70 per night.

For budget travelers, **Skiathos Blu Lodge** offers another appealing selection. Nestled within the Troulos Beach resort, merely a 10-minute drive from Skiathos Town, this establishment boasts a pool, bar, and restaurant. The rooms provide ample space and comprehensive amenities, with nightly prices spanning from €60 to €80.

Boudouriania Cottage stands as a charming guesthouse positioned in the enchanting village of Boudouriani. An optimal choice for frugal explorers desiring an authentic Greek island experience. The guesthouse encompasses a pool, garden, and barbecue area. The accommodations maintain simplicity and tidiness, ensuring comfort, at a rate of €50 to €70 per night.

Sunset Studios & Apartments suits budget travelers who seek proximity to the shoreline. Positioned in the Koukounaries beach resort, approximately a 15-minute drive from Skiathos Town, these commodious studios and apartments come equipped with ample facilities. Prices per nightfall are within the €60 to €80 range.

Classic budget lodging, **Hotel Australia**, can be found within Skiathos Town. Perfect for economical travelers craving accessibility to various activities, this hotel offers a pool, bar, and restaurant. The accommodations, although basic, exude cleanliness and comfort, priced between €50 and €70 per night.

Nestled in the village of Troulos, **Stelinia Inn** offers affordable lodging for those wishing to stay near the coastline. The hotel includes a pool, bar, and restaurant, while the rooms, though simple, are tidy and cozy. The rates stand at €50 to €70 per night.

Thymi's Home Hotel, situated in Tsoukalia village, embodies the allure of authentic Greek island life, catering to budget-conscious travelers. With a pool, garden, and barbecue area, the guesthouse provides a serene atmosphere. The accommodations offer simplicity paired with cleanliness and comfort, priced between €50 and €70 per night.

Muses Inn stands as an attractive option for budget travelers drawn to beach proximity. Nestled within the Koukounaries beach resort, approximately a 15-minute drive from Skiathos Town, this hotel offers a pool, bar, and restaurant. The rooms boast spaciousness and comprehensive amenities, with nightly prices ranging from €60 to €80.

Hotel Kostis, a modest budget establishment located in Skiathos Town, caters to economical travelers desiring convenience. The hotel features a pool, bar, and restaurant, while the accommodations, although basic, ensure cleanliness and comfort. Rates span from €50 to €70 per night.

Hotel Telis is an optimal choice for budget travelers seeking beachside accommodations. Situated in the Agia Paraskevi beach resort, around a 20-minute drive from Skiathos Town, this hotel boasts a pool, bar, and restaurant. The rooms offer spaciousness and extensive amenities, with prices per night falling within the €60 to €80 range.

Luxury Hotels and Resorts

Kassandra Shores Resort & Spa stands as a high-end spa retreat, offering elegant rooms and suites, as well as two pools, a secluded beach area, and dining options. Rates begin at €200 per night.

The Enigma Skiathos Luxury Residence presents an opulent collection of villas, each featuring private pools, sun terraces, and breathtaking ocean vistas. Prices commence at €250 per night.

Core Prestige Suites emerges as a refined establishment showcasing stylish suites, accompanied by a rooftop pool and spa amenities. Starting rates are set at €200 per night.

Skyline Sea Retreat Skiathos represents a contemporary resort boasting commodious rooms, a private beach, and an enjoyable water park. Prices begin at €150 per night.

ALTHAEA EXCLUSIVE ROOMS surfaces as a boutique hotel offering fashionable accommodations, complete with a rooftop pool and scenic sea views. Rates commence at €200 per night.

La Piscine Art Hotel, a part of the Philian Collection, embodies a sophisticated lodging option, characterized by art-adorned rooms, a pool, and a restaurant. Prices initiate at €250 per night.

Bourtzi Heritage Hotel stands as a historic establishment, complete with a lavish spa, private beach access, and captivating panoramic views. Prices commence at €300 per night.

Skiathos Avaton Hotel, a proud member of Philian Hotels & Resorts, represents a lavish hotel providing expansive rooms, spa facilities, and exclusive beach access. Starting rates are set at €350 per night.

Skiathos Princess Resort emerges as a family-oriented destination, featuring four pools, a water park, and a private beach. Prices start from €180 per night.

Elixia Skiathos Retreat stands as a wellness-focused resort offering a spa, fitness center, and private beach access. Prices commence at €250 per night.

Camping and Alternative Accommodations

Skiathos Campgrounds present an excellent choice for economical travelers yearning to embrace the outdoors. Nestled within the lush hills of Skiathos, roughly a 15-minute drive from the coastline, this camping site features a swimming pool, a playground, and a bar. Camping spots are available from €15 per night.

Skiathos Countryside Farm Camp introduces a functional farm setting that offers both camping and glamping encounters. Situated amidst the tranquil countryside of Skiathos, around a 20-minute drive from the shore, this farm establishment boasts a swimming pool, a playground, and a dining venue. Camping spaces begin at €20 per night, while glamping tents can be enjoyed starting from €50 per night.

Skiathos Sustainable Retreat is a petite, family-owned campsite dedicated to promoting eco-friendly tourism. Nestled within the pine-clad forests of Skiathos, approximately a 25-minute drive from the beach, this campsite offers a swimming pool, a playground, and a bar. Camping pitches are available starting from €25 per night.

Skiathos Hillside Bungalows presents a cluster of charming bungalows tucked within the elevated reaches of Skiathos, around a 30-minute drive from the coastline. These self-contained bungalows feature a kitchenette, a bathroom, and a terrace. Bungalows are accessible from €50 per night.

Skiathos Studio Residences offers a collection of well-appointed studios situated in the village of Mandraki, approximately a 35-minute drive from the beach. These self-sufficient studios comprise a kitchenette, a bathroom, and a balcony. Studio accommodations are available from €40 per night.

Skiathos Urban Apartments showcases a set of comfortable apartments situated in the village of Troulos, around a 40-minute drive from the beach. These self-catering apartments include a kitchen, a bathroom, and a balcony. Apartment stays commence from €60 per night.

Skiathos Country Villas features a collection of exquisite villas positioned within the serene countryside of Skiathos, about a 45-minute drive from the coastline. These self-contained villas offer a kitchen, a bathroom, a private swimming pool, and a terrace. Villa experiences begin at €100 per night.

Skiathos Woodland Treehouses offers a distinctive accommodation option, inviting guests to slumber within charming treehouses. Nestled within the tranquil woods of Skiathos, roughly a 50-minute drive from the beach, these treehouses boast a kitchenette, a bathroom, and a terrace. Treehouse lodgings are accessible from €150 per night.

Skiathos Nomadic Yurts provides another distinct lodging experience, inviting guests to reside within cozy yurts. Nestled within the rolling hills of Skiathos, around a 55-minute drive from the beach, these yurts are equipped with a kitchenette, a bathroom, and a terrace. Yurt stays commence from €200 per night.

BEST TRAVEL RESOURCES

These are the best travel resources I usually use:

SkyScanner: This is my favorite flight search engine of all time. It always appears to discover the greatest rates, and its calendar display shows you when days are the most affordable to travel. It appeals to me since it searches little booking sites that no one else does. Begin all of your flight searches here.

Momodo: This fantastic website searches a wide range of airlines, including several low-cost carriers that bigger sites overlook. While I usually start with Skyscanner, I'll also look at this site to compare costs.

Google Flights: Google Flights allows you to input your departure airport and view flights all around the globe on a map to get the cheapest destination. It's a useful search engine for learning about routes, connections, and prices.

Hostelworld: The market's most user-friendly hostel website, with the greatest inventory, the finest search interface, and the most availability. You may also look for private rooms or dorm beds. I use it for my reservations.

Couchsurfing: This website enables you to stay for free on people's sofas or in their spare rooms. It's a terrific way to save money while meeting locals who can teach you a lot more about a place than a hostel or hotel can. There are also groups on the web where you can organize to meet up for activities in your location.

Booking.com: Booking.com is an excellent resource for low-cost hotels and other forms of lodging. I enjoy how simple its UI is.

Trusted Housesitters: Try house- or pet-sitting for a novel (and free) way to travel. You just care after someone's home and/or pet while they are gone in return for free lodging. It's an excellent choice for long-term travelers and those on a tight budget.

CONCLUSION

In closing, Skiathos is truly a paradise waiting to be explored. This travel guide has been a journey through the myriad wonders that this Greek gem has to offer, from its pristine beaches to its charming villages, and from its delectable cuisine to its vibrant nightlife. But beyond the surface, there's an essence to Skiathos that's hard to capture in words alone.

As you reflect on the experiences and recommendations shared in this guide, remember that Skiathos is not just a destination; it's an invitation to immerse yourself in a world where time seems to slow down, and where the worries of the everyday fade away against the backdrop of the Aegean Sea.

Whether you're a sun seeker looking to bask on the golden sands, an adventurer seeking hidden coves and sea caves, or a culture enthusiast eager to explore historic sites and traditional villages, Skiathos caters to your every whim. It's a place where every day can be an adventure, whether you're traversing hiking trails, discovering local art, or indulging in the flavors of authentic Greek cuisine.

But beyond the activities and sights, Skiathos offers something intangible yet immensely powerful – a sense of connection. The warmth of the locals, the welcoming spirit of the island, and the genuine smiles that greet you at every corner create an atmosphere that feels like home, even if you've just arrived. It's this sense of community, of sharing moments with both locals and fellow travelers, that adds an extra layer of richness to your journey.

As you bid adieu to this sun-kissed haven, you'll find yourself carrying more than just souvenirs in your luggage. You'll carry memories of sunsets that painted the sky in breathtaking hues, of laughter, shared over delicious meals, and of the feeling of saltwater on your skin after a day spent in the embrace of the Aegean Sea.

So, whether you're planning a solo escape, a romantic getaway, or a family adventure, Skiathos beckons with open arms. It's a destination that encourages you to slow down, to savor every moment, and to embrace the simple pleasures of life. As you leave the island, you'll find that Skiathos has left an indelible mark on your heart, one that will stay with you long after your tan fades and your suitcase is unpacked.

Skiathos is more than just a place on the map; it's an experience that lingers in your soul. So, as you embark on your journey to this enchanting island, may your days be filled with sun-soaked memories, your nights with laughter, and your heart with the magic that only Skiathos can bestow.

Printed in Great Britain
by Amazon